Mathew Lyons is a freelance journalist and writer based in London. Graduating from university with a BA (Hons) in English and an MA in Renaissance literature, he has worked in legal and business publishing, writing several books in the process, as well as editing and contributing to a number of magazines. Most recently, he has written for *The Times* and *The Guardian*.

There and Back Again

For Helen,
Isaac and Evie,
with love

There and Back Again

in the footsteps of
J.R.R. Tolkien

Mathew Lyons

Published by Cadogan Guides 2004

Cadogan Guides
Highlands House, 165 The Broadway, Wimbledon, London SW19 1NE
info@cadoganguides.co.uk
www.cadoganguides.com

The Globe Pequot Press
246 Goose Lane, PO Box 480, Guilford,
Connecticut 06437–0480

Printed in Finland by WS Bookwell
A catalogue record for this book is available
from the British Library
ISBN 1-86011-139-4

Contents

Introduction

All in all I was relieved when, aged about 18, I stopped feeling the urge to reread *The Lord of the Rings*. I don't remember precisely when it happened. Like a favourite place that you go to everyday I think eventually it came to seem stale, dulled by familiarity, a secret I no longer cared to hold. I had read and re-read it – and to a much lesser degree *The Hobbit* – obsessively for 10 or so years. I had read Tolkien's other works, too, to the extent that they had been published then, in the late 1970s and early 1980s, but it was really only *The Lord of the Rings* that held me rapt. By my late teens I was definitely already feeling that it was a slight embarrassment, like admitting to still having a comfort blanket. It reminded me of my childhood and, since I was by now an adult – at least I thought so at the time – I was pleased to leave it behind.

There it lay, almost forgotten, at the very back of my mind for the next 10 to 15 years. I began to notice, however, towards the end of the 1990s, that a liking for Tolkien was slowly nudging its way towards respectability. When I had been reading him, it was unthinkable that anyone with pretensions to 'serious' literary taste could also countenance a liking for *The Lord of the Rings*. Not only was it a genre piece with no basis in the real world, but it featured ridiculous, quasi-human creatures, not to mention wizards, monsters and elves, and was written in a style that veered between faux archaisms and Edwardian bourgeois social comedy. W.H. Auden had probably been the only critic of any credibility to support it.

Yet I now heard people who certainly took their own literary credentials very seriously, not only admitting to having read it, but confessing to having been as caught up by it as I had been. (I use the word 'confess' advisedly: no one wanted to be tainted by the sin of bad taste.) I discovered that the trajectory of my relationship with *The Lord of the Rings*, from obsession through rejection to indifference, was a common one. Peter Jackson's hugely successful films, even before the first instalment had been released, pushed Tolkien yet further towards the mainstream. Soon I was hearing people – including, to my surprise, a close friend – freely admit to still reading it regularly. One acquaintance claimed to have read it over a hundred times. I, however, was still in a kind of denial, not wanting to accept the large part it had played in my adolescent life.

I began to wonder about my compulsion towards *The Lord of the Rings* as a teenager, what it had really been based on, what it was about the book that had snared me so completely. There was another, more personal development that made me look back too: I became a father. My children are still very young, under five, but watching their fascinations and tastes emerge, each new delight fresh-minted for them, the slightest story a joy, I thought more about my own childhood and what that experience of discovery had been like, wading out into the bright cold world.

I was 35 when I read *The Lord of the Rings* again. It was, I was relieved to find, a very different book from the one I remembered: sadder, darker, steeped in loss. I had forgotten a lot of the detail, but the narrative pull was as strong as ever, only now I saw clearly an undertow of sorrow and regret. If part of its appeal when I first encountered it was its completeness, its solipsism, then what I came across now was a more fractured, complex thing, with holds on the real world I had never imagined – or, more accurately, never noticed.

Reflecting on the way I engaged with his work, then and now, I became increasingly interested in Tolkien's own motivation and inspiration. It seems strange that I had never considered such things before, but I think I must have simply blocked out the emotional core of the book, blocked out, in fact, its meaning, to revel in the richness of the invention for its own sake. Insofar as I had conceived Tolkien's intentions when I read the book as an adolescent, I had seen it as an intellectual game, rooted in ancient literary sources. Clearly, language was vital to Tolkien too, though still, I thought, at the level of play. He rarely lost an opportunity to tell a correspondent or interviewer that linguistic invention came first for him and that the stories were merely there to flesh out what he called his secret vice.

A great deal has been written about Tolkien, but there are actually few books that – to my mind at least – offer genuine insight into his life and work. It seems reasonably well-established that Tolkien did not like people enquiring too deeply into his inspirations. Like many writers, he felt that biographically based criticism, as well as being intrusive and sometimes downright impertinent, also belittled both the work and the craft of writing.

Perhaps consequently, the definitive heavyweight biography has yet to be written, despite the wealth of personal documents, in the shape of diaries and letters, which survive. Of the biographies currently available, *J.R.R. Tolkien: A Biography* by Humphrey Carpenter is by far the best in terms of detail, balance and sympathetic insight into Tolkien's character. For the way in which he thought about his writing and the tools he used to achieve his ends, Tom Shippey's two books, *The Road to Middle Earth* and its more accessible revision, *J.R.R. Tolkien: Author of the Century*, are invaluable. Then there is the superb 12-volume *History of Middle Earth*, edited by Tolkien's youngest son and literary executor, Christopher, which, using hitherto unpublished manuscripts and drafts, charts the development of Tolkien's mythology from its beginnings in 1917 through to his death in 1973.

Through reading these books and others, as well as the volume of Tolkien's letters jointly edited by Humphrey Carpenter and Christopher Tolkien, I realized that language and literature were only two aspects of Tolkien's inspiration. Most notable, I discovered, was the desire to create a mythology for England, to take the poor remnants of Anglo-Saxon and other folk tales and myths, all but strangled by the imposition of Latinate French culture following the Norman Conquest, and make something whole again. He articulated this desire clearly in his letters, recalling the sense of grief he had felt as a young man when comparing the rich inheritance of the Finnish and Icelandic peoples, say, to that of the English. It nourished in him the extraordinary ambition to fill the gap himself, weaving a vast tapestry of legends and tales that would reflect the temperate clime and culture of his country,

England, to which the whole work would be dedicated.[1]

Then came the questions. If England, with its lost histories and changed landscapes, is his subject, where does it figure, precisely, in Middle Earth? Which places in England were important to him? Which did he celebrate? Which were among his inspirations?

There are no easy or systematic answers. Tolkien didn't give much away himself. Indeed, he was noticeably chary about making any explicit identifications between real places and those he created in his books. It is quite apposite, in fact, that the answers to those questions should be fragmentary and oblique.[2]

I began to conceive the idea of a journey through Tolkien's England, beginning in autumn 2002 and spread throughout the following year, to try to discover how he related his extraordinary creation to his beloved country, to reconnect him to the landscapes he was inspired by, whether directly or indirectly. Some locations, based on what I knew of his life by way of Carpenter's biography, seemed essential: the Warwickshire of his childhood, in particular Sarehole to the south of Birmingham; Oxford, where he lived most of his adult life, and a number of other places in the surrounding county; and places he was stationed during the First World War, such as Great Haywood in Staffordshire and Roos on the Yorkshire coast. He lived in Leeds, too, for a few years, but I know Leeds quite well, having lived there myself, and I failed to think of any substantive connection to Tolkien's fictional world.

There were several places that Tolkien visited briefly, whether in his professional capacity or simply on holiday, and that also seemed promising from what I had read, from Lancashire's Ribble Valley, to the Lizard in Cornwall, by way of Lydney Park in

Gloucestershire and the Berkshire Downs. Finally there were a handful of sites that could be linked with places in Middle Earth: The Cheddar Gorge in Somerset; the Buckinghamshire village of Brill; Fonthill in Wiltshire. Perhaps some of these links were tenuous; perhaps others would simply illuminate nothing. Either way I intended to find out.

No doubt there is room for argument about my choices. I certainly wouldn't pretend that my criteria were either rigorous or rigid. I intended to focus more on possible connections to *The Lord of the Rings* rather than those that, like Great Haywood, are linked to more obscure parts of his work. Mostly that simply reflects my personal prejudice. It was my journey, after all. I also intended to avoid visiting endless English villages simply because, like Buckland or Bucklebury, Tolkien made use of their name. There are, in any event, 15 Bucklands in England. They couldn't all have inspired him. Indeed, anyone who picks up a map of England, particularly if it focuses on the West Midlands, can't help but notice how much Tolkien borrowed from real places for his nomenclature. English place names were undoubtedly of interest to him, but it was the names rather than the places that absorbed his attention.

What I set out to do, then, was less to map Middle Earth onto contemporary England and give Ordnance Survey grid references for the Fords of Bruinen or the Dimrill Stair, and more to search for the origins of ideas. I was looking for places that, whether because of their natural beauty or their histories or their emotional significance to him, became charged with creative meaning for him. While the world that finally emerged into print in *The*

Hobbit and *The Lord of the Rings* is obviously central, I was still interested in the ghosts that lay beneath it, as much for Tolkien's evolving approach to England as for the places themselves. There were innumerable layers to pick apart, from the early *Book of Lost Tales*, through the first drafts of *The Silmarillion* in the 1920s, to *The Lost Road* of the early 1930s and *The Notion Club Papers* some 10 years later. The relationship of all these writings to England, or to ideas of England, can shed a great deal of light on the way Tolkien thought and felt about his country, and how he sought to memorialize it in the extraordinary and original way he did.

In spite of the fact that one of his major themes in *The Lord of the Rings* is man's capacity for the unnecessary and brutal despoiling of the natural landscape, most such places can still be visited. Some, certainly, have changed, and not always for the better. Yet there are many locations in England where you can look around and see largely what he would have seen, and wonder at what such landscapes actually meant to him and how they reflected his concerns back at him.

I hope in the course of this book to offer some idea of the texture of the England that Tolkien wished to celebrate: its landscape, its history, its language. I hope, too, to convey the extent to which the last two categories are always present when we stand and look out across England. It is, I think, a distinct way of viewing the country: trying to loosen our focus on what presents itself today and instead see the sway of history like a shadow passing over the fields, to hold in view not only the landscape, but Tolkien himself, his work and his interests, working out the relationships between them all.

Certainly, some of those relationships are surprising. One of the many shocks that lay in store for aficionados in the publication of the *History of Middle Earth* was that Tolkien's declaration of intent to create a body of myth for England was in origin entirely literal. The Shire may have seemed to us previously a direct enough reflection of his ardour for his homeland, but while it is a homage it is also a caricature. For all their spirit and bucolic *joie de vivre*, hobbits are narrow-minded and self-absorbed, weak, almost xenophobic on occasion. If the Shire is particularly favoured, it is because its land is fertile and its inhabitants have been too insignificant to catch the eye of Sauron before.

However, in the very first versions of his myths, in *The Book of Lost Tales*, Tolkien made the land of the Elves England itself, often explicitly so. Eriol, the first of Tolkien's many wandering characters mediating between the mortal and immortal worlds, comes to Tol Eressëa across the North Sea. When he arrives he is renamed Angol by the elves, a clear echo of the Angles from what is now Schleswig, from whom the word 'England' is derived. In later drafts Tol Eressëa begins in the Far West but is dragged back east into the position of England, with Ireland breaking away. By the time Tolkien abandoned the conceit altogether in the 1920s, England had a double role: it was both the land from which the Elves set sail when they departed the world of men, and for which they have a particular love, and also the place from which the wandering Eriol figure, by now renamed Aelfwine, hales. England was at this point called Luthany, Leithian or Lúthien. These last two names clearly echo that of Lúthien Tinuviel, who was herself inspired by Tolkien's wife Edith; the long poem Tolkien composed on the subject of Lúthien's love for Beren is called 'The Lay of Leithian'.

Even after this line of thought had been set aside, Tolkien was clearly still striving to find a way to place England on his maps and in his tales without ambiguity. It becomes the Western Isles in the *Quenta* of c.1930, a part of what remained after the drowning of Beleriand. Indeed, Tolkien toyed with the idea of naming Beleriand Ingolondë instead.[3]

The essential idea underlying all of this effort is that, by virtue of its close association with elvendom, it is England alone that has the 'true' tales from that perilous realm, the true history of the elves (albeit throughout all this, Tolkien was still sticking, inexplicably as it seems now, to the word 'gnomes'), while those handed down through other nations are little more than garbled nothings. It is of course demonstrably true that the tales Tolkien was collecting were nothing like anything in a genuine folkloric tradition, despite having more in common with the Scandinavian and Germanic than most. The ubiquity of Middle Earth and *The Lord of the Rings* today blinds us to the novelty of what Tolkien was actually trying to do: to weld the cold, bleak ethics and action of the northern mythic tales onto the popular domestic tradition, however attenuated, of elves, goblins and dwarves – with a dash of Anglo-Saxon literary culture thrown in for good measure.

Tolkien did not invent the genre. He was profoundly influenced by, for instance, the heroic romances of William Morris, such as *The Roots of the Mountains* or *The House of the Wolfings*, as well as by Morris's translations of the Icelandic sagas. Yet no one had set out to achieve anything of the breadth and depth of Middle Earth, and certainly not with Tolkien's knowledge of literary and linguistic sources in early northern Europe.

Aside from that, Tolkien's early drafts also have transparently personal elements that make one wonder whether there might be more such autobiographical echoes as yet unheard and undiscovered in his later works too. The most obvious of these in *The Book of Lost Tales* concerns the two cities of the Elves, Tavrobel and Kortirion, which are, as we can see from Tolkien's notes, based on Great Haywood in Staffordshire and the county town of Warwick to the south. Oxford, too, was later brought into the myth, as Taruithorn. All three featured heavily in the landscape of Tolkien's relationship with his wife, Ethel. Oxford was where Tolkien had studied and also where he worked, barring a few years at Leeds in the early 1920s, for the rest of his life. He was stationed periodically at Great Haywood during the First World War; it was there that he first drafted some of the tales that eventually appeared in *The Silmarillion* some 60 years later. Ethel, wanting to be, if not close by, then at least reasonably accessible, moved to Warwick, 40 miles to the southeast and the other side of Birmingham.

Moreover, Tolkien was happy to introduce more specific concordances with contemporary England into his work. There is a House of the Hundred Chimneys at Tavrobel, which appears in 'The Tale of the Sun and Moon', and which seems almost certainly a reference to the great country house of Shugborough in Great Haywood. Shugborough may not have quite 100 chimneys, but it certainly has 80. Both Great Haywood and Tavrobel can boast a bridge where two rivers meet: Tavrobel has the Gruir and the Afros; Great Haywood, the Trent and the Sow.

It is easy for us to look back from the comfort of hindsight and see how unlikely Tolkien was to succeed in what he was trying to achieve here. Part of the problem, I think, is that Tolkien still hadn't really shaken off all the less palatable trappings of 'the land of faërie'. We should probably ignore his preference for the word 'gnomes', alongside or instead of 'elves', which he retained until surprisingly late. After all, part of the reason the latter seems more preferable is probably simply that it is more familiar now after his successful use of it. Gnomes might have sillier associations, but it is not as if elves had figured anywhere as anyone's idea of grace, wisdom and nobility before Tolkien's intervention. They were usually being more concerned to frolic among the flowers of the field, bewitching cattle and generally making a nuisance of themselves. Yet he was still given to describing his creations collectively with terms such as 'Holy Companies', although sometimes the companies are lonely or bright, too, and there are far too many tinkling dances on the green and the like, even one being too many, in my view. Moreover, he was evidently fond of turning descriptive phrases into nouns – the Throne of Hate or the Room of Logs – which, if anything, subtracts from any inherent seriousness.

Even Tolkien's most ardent fans are likely to feel that his early work, for all its academic interest, does not necessarily show his aesthetic judgements in their best light. He clearly thought that Tinfang Warble was a good name, for instance, sticking with it for years and even going so far as to write two poems on the subject, at least one of which is breathtakingly unsuccessful.[4] The very earliest sketch of the figure that emerged as Sauron the Terrible was Tevildo, Prince of Cats.

Notwithstanding these problems, however, it was for the most part the framing device he had most trouble with, the transmission of the tales from his beloved archaic past to the present. It is into these that he built most of his explicit references to England and the English. It is fairly clear, from the frequent and thorough revisions and rewritings these were subjected to, that he knew that they weren't working and were, in fact, failing to really articulate what it was he loved about his country, whether its landscape, its people or its language. Perhaps he felt that his histories of the elves, tragic and heroic as they are, should be enough to celebrate England by the way he associated them with this island. However, I suspect he knew that it wasn't enough, neither subtle enough nor explicit enough. He would have to find a way of doing it whereby England was in the very bones of the earth, yet overlay the forests and fields, too. It would take him decades to discover how.

Chapter One
A personal journey

I have of course thrown it all away, all the evidence of my teenage Tolkien obsession, and recently, too, certainly in the last five years. It simply felt like baggage, like ill-fitting clothes. My compulsion never extended much beyond books, either. I was never particularly drawn to the idea of donning pointy shoes and a cape, either as part of some role-playing gathering or, for that matter, in the privacy of my bedroom. The books alone were enough to mark me out as an addict. My clear-out saw me discard pretty much anything of Tolkien's that was in print between, say, 1974 and 1982: not just *The Lord of the Rings*, *The Hobbit* and *The Silmarillion*, but *Farmer Giles of Ham*, *Tree and Leaf*, *The Adventures of Tom Bombadil* and *Unfinished Tales*, which, at one time, I'd been inordinately proud of, as one of the first hard-backed books I'd ever owned. Out went *The Tolkien Compass*, *The Complete Guide to Middle Earth*, *The Master of Middle Earth* and many others. Out, too, much to my surprise now, went *An Introduction to Elvish*[1] and a copy of *La Communauté de l'Anneau*, which, as any self-respecting Tolkien zealot will tell you, is a French translation of *The*

Fellowship of the Ring. I say surprise because, looking back, it is hard to comprehend why I would have wanted to buy them in the first place.

Even at the time, I think, I half-felt that these last two were a step too far. They weren't the sort of things I wanted friends to know I owned. I hid them away on high, inaccessible shelves, out of bounds to curious bedroom visitors. Strangely, I can picture these two books far more vividly than I can many of the others. *An Introduction to Elvish* had a one-colour jacket, a vivid St Patrick's Day green with some kind of white, spider-webby design on the front; the binding was thick and unyielding, but the paper was crisp and white. *La Communauté de l'Anneau* was a sombre burgundy, in a small format, with type closely spaced in that style so beloved of the French, at once old-fashioned and difficult to read. Not that I'm making any excuses for failing to get much past the first paragraph. I had bought it thinking that working my way through it might be a pleasurable way to improve my French. Sadly, such high romantic ideals crumpled at their first encounter with my basic lack of skill in the language – actually in any language – and a deeply ingrained inertia.

I used to have frequent, if brief, bursts of seeking self-improvement like that, especially when there might be some kind of intellectual cachet in it. I wanted to be the sort of 15-year-old who had already read *Finnegans Wake* (I reached the top of page 2) or *War and Peace* (I'm not sure I even finished the first paragraph) or J.G. Ballard's *Crash* (I didn't get past the cover of this – my mum confiscated it on the basis of an absurd prejudice against the eroticization of car crashes). I certainly adored the *idea* of linguistic facility, the ability to learn Latin or Greek – since my local school offered neither – and read Sappho or Lucretius, Homer or Virgil in the original. Not that I'd read them in English. The *Teach Yourself...* books on Latin and Modern Greek lay on my shelf no more thumbed than they'd been in W.H. Smiths at Brent Cross Shopping Centre ('in London's North West End', the adverts said) as I mulled their purchase, probably trying to weigh up the likelihood of my actually using them against the intellectual kudos of owning them in the first place. Learning languages, I had discovered to my dismay, was all too much like science – all those conjugations and cases to memorize. Who knew that languages had cases? I certainly didn't. I didn't even understand what cases were. Being educated in the 1970s, I had no formal understanding of grammar at all.

Tolkien would not have approved of such ignorance, I have no doubt. It wasn't just that he had a talent for languages, although he certainly did. It was that he found in them, in their structures as much as their sounds, an aesthetic satisfaction that I simply cannot comprehend. It seems to have been a sensory pleasure for him, a kind of synaesthesia. His depth of knowledge was extraordinary, barely intelligible to someone with my indifference to even the common European languages, never mind the obscure, ancient or lost ones. He once told an evidently bemused interviewer that 'Of course, the Elvish language is deliberately made to follow to some extent the same type of changes that turned primitive Celtic into Welsh.'[2]

Why on Earth I thought a book on Elvish was a good idea, Heaven only knows. In most respects Tolkien sat in antithesis to all my adolescent pretensions. The sort of friends likely to be impressed by my reading *Finnegans Wake*, assuming that they hadn't got there first, were precisely those most likely to react with horror at the mention of anything as popular as *The Lord of the Rings*. Even I recognized that the mere idea of learning Elvish – I'm sorry to say that was as far as I ever got – was a pretty extreme manifestation of my compulsion. It was certainly the high-water mark. Looking back, however, I'm not sure I even connected my interest in Elvish with the insurmountable difficulties I had getting to grips with the most basic of phrases in other languages. It wasn't so much a language as a key to a more intimate understanding of *The Lord of the Rings*.

I think in fact it had more to do with the survival into adolescence of a desire for secrets for their own sake, a desire that derived from the discovery of privacy, an idea you happen across at a time when your parents still regard every second of your existence as something they have a right to share. At primary school, I know, my friends and I had a sequence of secret clubs, complete with rule books and passwords, badges and codes, that had no other purpose than to be secret and keep others out.

Middle Earth fed that desire for secrecy, too. It was, for me at least, but I think for most teenage readers at the time, a private world, something that was ours, shared between the faithful, and something that our parents, in particular, didn't understand. To this day my dad persists in the belief that Tolkien's books are set in outer space, an idea he found difficult to marry to my writing a travel book on the subject. Now that Tolkien is everywhere I suspect that this sense of ownership has become rather diluted, if it hasn't evaporated altogether. The urge to learn Elvish must have been fed by the same flame – it represented a secret code, something known only to the cognoscenti, the illuminati, an ersatz freemasonry, a sense of connection with unknown, like-minded people across the still vast distances of the world.

Perhaps at this point I should be a little more honest about my teenage Tolkien obsession. If my experience is anything to go by, *The Lord of the Rings* is a book that it's possible to like in general and re-read incessantly, while still finding large swathes of it entirely unsympathetic. This is an odd characteristic: it is hard to think of another writer sections of whose work his or her audience will happily ridicule while still retaining a fanatical loyalty to the whole.

It's not possible now to remember when I first read *The Lord of the Rings*, and certainly not the first time I read *The Hobbit*. I would guess that I read the latter when I was about seven and the former when I was about 10. I think I can remember lying on my bed in early evening sunlight, in the room I shared with my brother until I was about 11. Truth be told, we both shared it with the model railway that ate up a good half of the room, spreading out imperially across the plywood surface that my mum had built, a lovely plastic landscape of *papier mâché* hills and moulded tunnels, rudimentary home-made trees – the best of them done by my elder sister – and neat stations peopled with dapper figures from an age already gone: the women in smart coats, the men all bowler-hatted, except perhaps the odd blue-dungareed labourer, sleeves rolled up, bare-headed or bearing a blue worker's cap, vaguely Maoist now I think of it.

From the level of my bed you couldn't see the land as you lay, simply the complex structure of two-inch square pine supports beneath, like a rudimentary vaulted medieval church roof, or the struts between the wings on an Avro 504 biplane. Somehow I associate the pleasures of lying there reading with days off school sick with something minor, just enough to win you the benefit of the doubt, a mild stomach bug perhaps, which earned you buttery chicken sandwiches and fizzy lemonade. Although reading like this was occasionally furtive, it was never a guilty pleasure, but private and untroubled, the house clear of older siblings, the day stretching ahead like the open sea.

Books were always like that for me. Long after lights out in my room, itself a deadline generously extended, I lay awake at night reading by the landing light that came through my still open door, leaning out of bed to catch as much as possible on the open pages of the book, hiding it under my pillow, fingers holding the page, when footsteps rose up the staircase, practising the slow steady breath of a sleeping boy, listening out for the steps falling away again. I don't think I was fooling anyone and if I was going to lose my eyesight, as routinely suggested, well, there were worse ways for it to go.

I can remember re-reading *The Lord of the Rings* like that, half listening out for the click of the lounge door opening downstairs while my mind churned through the peoples to find characters to relate to, gorging on the geography, the places, the landscapes, wild and yet familiar, ancient but known. Specifically, I can remember imagining myself into the Prancing Pony at Bree when Aragorn enters the story. He inhabited for me the same world as

James Drury, who played the eponymous hero of *The Virginian* on Saturday morning TV. I can remember his black leather waistcoat, dark clothes and black hat impressing me – when I was aged maybe nine – as the epitome of some kind of cool. He didn't speak much. Aragorn, too, could be taciturn, masking an essential kindness and gentility in a show of brusque masculinity.

It seems strange, looking back, that, as someone with the standard-issue adolescent attraction to despair, loss and general hopelessness, I should have entirely missed the pervasive theme of the 'long defeat' that runs through *The Lord of the Rings*. I'd like to argue that you have to read it against the grain of the genre to find it, but I'm not sure I could get away with that. The sense of a fallen world, of greatness and beauty fading, of both death and immortality as kinds of curses: all of them are on more or less every page and should certainly have fed my taste for miserabilism, which on occasion shaded off into outright morbidity. I can certainly remember a phase of endless enquiry about people's modes of death. Surprisingly, I find I can date this pretty exactly, since I can remember being entirely absorbed by reading about the depression-related suicide of the English early music specialist David Munrow in my father's copy of the *London Evening Standard*. Not that I had heard of him. Munrow died on 15 May 1976 aged 33, when I was nine. There was a photo of him in the paper, as I recall, holding an instrument I didn't recognize, but of course it wasn't that fact that held my attention.

Mostly, I suspect, this derived from a fascination with what it might be like to die – particularly when, as with Munrow, it was self-inflicted – part of coming to terms with all the unknown things that lie on the other side of life. I was certainly afraid of death, becoming an avid hypochondriac, relating whatever stray facts about fatal illnesses I came across to my own, actually reasonably healthy, existence. I did have asthma and I did my best to parlay this into something dark and life-threatening, which, if it can be *in extremis*, it certainly wasn't in my case. Having read somewhere – or more likely heard on television – that an early sign of a heart attack is an arrhythmic beat I checked my pulse obsessively, especially when forced into rare bouts of physical exercise.

In some respects this is a kind of monstrous egotism, a solipsistic horror that the world could possibly exist without me in it. While not desirable in an adult, I'm not sure there's anything wrong with it in a child. In any case, in mitigation, I was brought up an atheist. I can certainly remember a genuine terror of personal oblivion, lying awake at night afraid to sleep in case the morning never came. This probably says more about me than it did about lack of religious faith, since I also used to lie awake and worry about vampires, pulling the duvet up around my face as a protection. Then of course there was nuclear war, which in the late 1970s and early 1980s felt to me at least a real prospect, a poisonous cloud of unknowing hovering over my future. It wasn't that abstract, either: there were public information films, Britain seemed to be rearming, Reagan's America was ratcheting up the pressure. I recently came across an old school notebook where, in answer to the question 'What will this area be like in 25 years?' I had written, no doubt much to the irritation of the teacher, 'It will probably be much the same if it isn't destroyed by nuclear war.' Looking back now I wonder if these kinds of fears were in part behind my obsessive reading, particularly when I used to do so long after I was in bed with the bedroom light out. Perhaps I read *The Lord of the Rings* as I did to escape from these small mostly domestic demons who possessed the dark corners of my room. I know I developed little superstitions of my own: that I couldn't die with a book, or sometimes even a chapter, unfinished. Or perhaps they were simply vast ontological excuses I made to myself so that I could carry on reading.

Reading *The Lord of the Rings* now as an adult, and as a parent too, I can still see the shape of my childhood, my adolescent delights, on the page, and remember the way I savoured them at each re-reading: Aragorn's introduction at the Prancing Pony, Gandalf's fall in Moria and the story of his resurrection, the Ents' destruction of Isengard, Lothlorien and the rest. (I can see, too, the first buds of such pleasures in my four-year-old son's thirst for stories about castles and dragons, even if in his case such stories must include firefighters too.) Yet it is the wider sense of defeat that I see most clearly now: the dying clamour of peoples whose lives have gone unrecorded, and whose sorrows and triumphs lie as deep as their enemies' beneath the indifferent earth. It is almost suffocating; I certainly think Tolkien found it so.

I probably read *The Lord of the Rings* at least twice a year through my adolescence, sometimes more, so often that the readings of it blurred. I do remember that I'd frequently turn to it as something to absorb myself with when I should have been revising for exams. No deadline was so pressing that it couldn't be postponed by a breeze through *The Lord of the Rings*. I think that early on I must have decided what I liked and didn't like about it, and simply skipped the bits I found tedious, even in some parts offensive. Certainly, by the time I got round to sitting important exams I could knock if off in a couple of days.

I made no attempt to rationalize to myself the sections I skipped over. Actually, that's not entirely true. I rationalized the habit by telling myself that I was just reading the good bits. With most other things I might have read and liked, I intellectualized endlessly and no doubt needlessly, but with Tolkien I was really only there for the ride. It was as if *The Lord of the Rings* existed in a different class of literature, not subject to the same criteria as other books, because my response – however else you might characterize it – was only emotional.

Prime among the scenes I expurgated as I raced through were any that involved Sam opening his mouth. Sam made my flesh crawl. It wasn't just that, raised in a good liberal/left household, I found his servility politically unacceptable, although I did. Even aged 10 I would have made that judgement. We were that kind of family. Nor was it simply that the physicality of his love for Frodo seemed oddly distasteful, unsettling – all that weeping and pawing. It was that you could pretty much guarantee that anything he contributed in the way of dialogue would either have a bilious folksy sententiousness or else be clearly meant to be endearingly foolish, the ramblings of a wise idiot.

There were quite a few things about the book that I reacted violently against, and most of them had to do with hobbits. Setting Sam aside, I simply didn't like them as a species (sub-species, whatever). Pippin and Merry, to my mind, were plain irritating, childish, puerile; Frodo was too earnest by half; the Gaffer and his ilk were irksome cartoons; all the stuff at the beginning about Bolgers and Proudfoots – sorry, Proudfeet – and the Sackville-Bagginses was dull and, worse, not funny. 'This is light comedy and light comedy is not Mr Tolkien's forte,' wrote Auden, with commendable understatement, in the *New York Times*. Now, clearly, that meant that I skipped at least a fifth of the book, maybe more. From the breaking of the fellowship onwards I used to ignore what I now think are probably the more meaningful parts of the book – those concerning bonding, duty and sacrifice – and concentrated on the walking trees, Tom Bombadil, the wild men of the woods and so on.

What else didn't I like? Gollum was always a nuisance, especially the studiously slimy way he spoke, as if we didn't know already that he wasn't one of us. He also reminded me of *The Hobbit*, which I had clearly liked when I first read it but had now decided was a mere children's book, and not a very good one at that – a particularly harsh and immature judgement. I can't say I was enamoured of the elves, either. To put it another way, I didn't really fall under the spell of their enchantment. I think, as with Sam, I felt coerced into accepting their wisdom and the beauty of, well just about everything about them, without really feeling it was justified. You could almost feel Tolkien rolling up his sleeves for some of the descriptions of their 'high' culture; you could certainly see him trying to cheat on several occasions by using the adjective 'elvish' as a shorthand for everything he was trying to convey about them but was presumably unable to articulate. I have a similar problem with the amount of work the adjective 'fair' is made to do in the book. I know it is meant to recall the literature of the medieval period, in particular the heroic romances, but its meaning – always vague and elusive – wears pretty thin with the degree of repetition it meets with. Of course, it is a commonplace criticism – from those who don't like the book – that Tolkien was a poor writer. All those archaisms. All those poems. Very unfashionable. It's not a view I share, although I grant there are weaknesses. The Scouring of the Shire is in fact my particular bugbear: he uses the word 'ruffian' some 32 times in 22 pages – yes, I did count them – sometimes as many as five times on the same page. It doesn't help that the word now is almost a museum piece, only dusted down when we want to satirize the world view of the upper classes. But it wasn't as if Tolkien had a small vocabulary, or as if he were on a deadline.

Given that I didn't like so much about the book – including four of the main characters – why did I carry on reading and re-reading? The easy answer is escapism. It's certainly the term most often applied to readers of the genre that has sprung up in Tolkien's wake – as indeed it is to most genre fiction. Of course Middle Earth and other fantasy worlds are places that enable the free outlet of thought and emotions in a way that 'real world' narratives, operating under a range of constraints, both narrative and stylistic, just don't. But 'escapism' is a pejorative term: I'm not sure that it is right. The kind of freedom offered by fantasy is, I think, by no means negative. Fantasy may transport you to worlds where dragons still sleep on their hoards beneath the mountains. To that extent it evidently takes you away from reality. But fantasy is also a mirror. Tom Shippey quotes an Anglo-Saxon proverb, 'Man does as he is when he may do as he wishes.'[3] Shippey applies it to the corrupting power of the Ring, but it may be applied equally to the experience of reading fantasy fiction. Precisely because it offers the reader so much imaginative licence – and surely that is true of Tolkien, more than most – it shows us or helps us to find out who we are.

To the extent that I knew who I was as a teenager, I would probably have defined myself by the books I read. Despite a fondness for intellectual posturing, I read everything I could lay my hands on. My instinct is to try and define myself by my reading: what kind of person was I when I read that first? I know that at the younger end of my Tolkien phase I read just about anything I could get my hands on. Contemporary with *The Lord of the Rings* when I first came across it would have been everything from Enid Blyton through to Rudyard Kipling, by way of John Masefield, Willard Price, Rosemary Sutcliff and C.S. Lewis, to name just a few. I might have been sneaking a peek at James Bond, borrowing my parents' stylish 1960s paperbacks when their backs were turned; maybe Sherlock Holmes and Brigadier Gerard too. I also had a taste for true-life stories. Perhaps it's obvious boy's stuff, but I read endless tales about pirates, highwaymen and outlaws, as well as 'great crime' books about, say, the Great Train Robbers. Leatherslade Farm, where they hid after the raid, is not far from Brill: I got a small thrill of recognition the moment I saw it on the map. In fact, I still have surprisingly vivid memories from all this: of the death of Jesse James, for instance, shot in the back by Robert Ford as he stood on a chair to hang a picture; of Ned Kelly's final stand in home-made armour and his last words on the gallows, 'Such is life'; of Dick Turpin, driving his horse to exhaustion and death by riding non-stop up the Great North Road to escape arrest.

I am wary of generalizing from my experience, but in what I remember of my reading – and of what I looked for in books – I think you can detect a clear thirst for otherness, for things that related to my everyday existence only by analogy, and often not even by that. I think it was Tolkien's great insight in *The Hobbit* and, particularly, *The Lord of the Rings*, to provide that sense of otherness, of difference, in a distant world that is still our world, albeit ours having become disfigured by time; a world that we can find vague, strange echoes of in our language and culture, that connects to us not through a journey through space or time, or across an ocean or through a doorway, but through the sensibility of the hobbits, which, for all their faults, is more like ours than it is like, say, Aragorn's; and, of course, through a sense of place.

Chapter Two
Beginnings and endings

It wasn't the best start. December found me stamping my feet in a vain attempt to keep warm, hunched against ice-cold rain billowing in heavy, misty sheets from low swollen clouds. I was on the Holderness peninsula in the East Riding of Yorkshire, just north of the Humber estuary and a few miles west of the North Sea. I was outside the small village of Roos looking for a small patch of woodland – and not only for shelter. Everywhere seemed a long way away, even Hull, a dozen or so miles to the southeast.

I hadn't been sure where to begin. There were, after all, a number of potential beginnings, among them Sarehole, where Tolkien lived as a child, and Oxford, where he spent most of his working life and wrote *The Lord of the Rings*. Yet Roos seemed to draw me somehow. This was partly because, even though I lived in Yorkshire for a number of years, the area around Hull was entirely unknown to me and I had almost no idea what to expect of the landscape, let alone Tolkien's connections with it. Partly, too, it was because Tolkien had been unusually explicit – and uniquely personal – in identifying it as a place of relevance to his work.

It was more than relevant: it was at its very heart. For Tolkien, the tale of Lúthien Tinúviel and Beren was the seed from which his mythology sprung. And that tale had its inspiration, he wrote, in a wood outside Roos.[1] It seems that Tolkien, though stationed at the Humber Garrison, was in fact on extended sick leave from the front. However, the evidence on the date is confused. Tolkien himself recalled it as being 1918. Edith had given birth to John, their first son, in Cheltenham on 16 November 1917 and they did not return north until after the christening. Tolkien stayed on the Humber until late spring 1918, according to Carpenter, when he was moved to Penkridge in Staffordshire. It is most likely, then, that the moment was some time in the spring of 1918. Christopher Tolkien, however, says that the first version of the story – 'The Tale of Tinúviel' – was begun in 1917.[2]

Tolkien's young wife Edith and their infant son John were staying in Roos. One evening, probably in spring, she had sung and danced for him through the woods in the twilight. It is a long way from this simple, conventional yet charming image to the actual story of Beren and Lúthien, which, like much of *The Silmarillion*, was reworked in many, sometimes radically different versions – Tom Shippey has identified at least eight retellings[3] – the most notable of which is probably the unfinished 'Lay of Leithian', a poem of more than 4,000 lines of rhyming couplets, written in the early 1930s. It was a story that Tolkien could not let go of, returning to it even as late as the 1970s. This isn't the place to sort through the various retellings, but at its core it is an Orphic tale, about a bond of love powerful enough to allow the elven Lúthien to follow the mortal Beren to the halls of the dead – that is, to allow her to lay down her immortality – and reclaim a brief time together for the two of them on Middle Earth before departing again.

Although one of Tolkien's favourite devices, that of love between the divided – he would probably have said sundered – species of man and elf, is present in some versions, and might in fact appear central, it was an imposition: it was early, but not *ab initio*. Aragorn relates a version of it to the hobbits before they are attacked by the Black Riders on Weathertop. I suspect that, at the time he wrote this passage, Tolkien was thinking that *The Silmarillion* would never see publication and that this might be his only chance to tell the story. It is revealing that the moment from the tale – in some versions several hundred pages long – that Tolkien chooses to emphasize by placing it at the beginning is the meeting of Beren and Lúthien, when he sees her dancing in the evening forest.

It wasn't so much the urge to identify the particular stretch of woodland that brought me to Roos, although I'll admit that that was at the back of my mind too. It was more to understand a little better what it might have been like for the young parents to be here three years into the Great War, with Tolkien due back on active service when he recovered his health.

Roos itself, I suspect, is largely unchanged from the village they knew. Its area now is not much greater than the space it occupied on an Ordnance Survey map of 1904; there is a little obviously 20th-century building, but not much. I would guess that most of the houses date from the 19th century, a few even earlier.

I had driven up from London, arriving in the early afternoon.

The whole of England south of the Humber had been consumed by mist and rain; here it had been little better, as I had discovered on my first attempt to scout around, but, as the afternoon drew on and the daylight faded, the weather calmed a little and the rain began to lift. We were a few days shy of the winter equinox. By mid-afternoon the light was already dying. Across the flat green fields of the peninsula the trees and hedgerows that marked their borders seemed no more than charcoal smudges against the sky, or careless fingerprints. Much of the land here was once inter-tidal, and has been reclaimed from the sea with the network of drains and dykes that crisscross the area. It's a very open landscape, with few natural features to draw the eye. Even though it is not visible from a distance, it is the Humber itself that dominates, not just because of the suspension bridge or the port or the industrial estates that line its shores, but also because its mass of water, shining like beaten metal even on a dismal day like this, seems to define something of the land's character, a reminder that the sea could take back these fields at any time.

The estuary has dominated its history too. Its port has long been important; the garrison at which Tolkien was stationed dates back hundreds of years for just that reason. Further back still, the Danes used it to raid deep into Saxon England in the 10th century. Indeed, many place names in the area reveal Scandinavian origins. One such, about 30 miles to the northwest of Roos, is the village of Wetwang, which probably means 'wet field'. When Tolkien borrowed the name for *The Lord of the Rings* he quite rightly made it apply to an area of fenland, much like that on the Holderness peninsula would have been before it was reclaimed. In doing this he is almost correcting reality. Usually, when place names clearly refer to elements of landscape, they do so accurately; it would be perverse for them to do otherwise. Yorkshire's Wetwang is an anomaly, therefore, since the land around it has never been particularly marshy.[4]

There are other, less direct echoes of Middle Earth in the place names of this part of Yorkshire. Tolkien notes that hobbit names such as Frodo or Bilbo have changed a little in translation; in 'reality' they ended in 'a', hence Froda. Froda, in fact, is a Germanic king who is mentioned in passing in *Beowulf*. His name survives in North Frodingham to the east of Hornsea, itself north of Roos.

By the time I was able to explore the area around Roos the light was fading fast. The low clouds overhead were dark as a bruise and bearing down; all around on the horizon they burned white. For all that the rain had gone, the wind was still blasting remorselessly in from the east, singing through the telephone cables above. I discovered that there were three or four small patches of woodland in which Tolkien and his wife could have walked, mostly to the south of the village. Their time must have been circumscribed by his ongoing, if low-level, military duties and the needs of their baby son John, no more than six months old, who lived with Edith in her lodgings. I doubt that they strayed too far. Slightly disappointingly, if predictably, it was impossible to know which grove Tolkien was referring to. It was, ironically, twilight now. I had originally thought the copse just outside the village might have been the one, but it seemed too close, not sufficiently private. Perhaps it was the covert a little further south, towards Winestead. I walked down the dark unlit road, untroubled by cars. Through the trees I could see the black towers of an oil refinery some miles away burning off the excess gas, the garish orange flares lighting up the horizon like vast torches, bouncing a strange, ominous light off the low cloud above. It was not, I imagine, a view that Tolkien would have much enjoyed.

The vision in a twilit glade, Beren happening upon Lúthien by chance and being inspired to love: these appear in each version of their story that Tolkien wrote. It is a small epiphany to which the sense of place is the key. It is not simply the dance or the song or the movement of the moonlight on the folds of Edith's dress, it is the moths and the branches of the trees, the white flowers of the hemlock, the chestnuts and the elms: nature stilled by love, held by beauty. The temptation is to assume that what made the moment so memorable for Tolkien was that when he saw Edith dance it, too, was a defining moment in the early days of their relationship. Yet nothing could be further from the truth.

Ronald – his preferred Christian name – had first met Edith, at 19 three years his senior, when they were in lodgings together in Birmingham 10 years earlier, in 1908. Ronald and his younger brother Hilary had been orphaned and were in the care of the Catholic Church; she was also orphaned, in addition to being illegitimate. When love blossomed it is perhaps understandable that his guardian, Father Francis Morgan, was horrified. But when he forbade the two to have any contact, let alone see one another, until Tolkien's 21st birthday, he was doing the worst possible thing. Indeed, as Tolkien acknowledged many years later (*Letters*, p53), it was probably the only thing that could have turned a teenage infatuation into something more solid and lasting. He wrote to Edith the day he came into his majority in 1913. Within a week they were engaged and debating a further obstacle: that he was Catholic and she was not.

What, then, gave this moment in Roos such significance? I think the answer lies in the pressure of circumstances. Despite the birth of John in November 1917, Ronald and Edith had actually spent little time together as a married couple. He was already commissioned by the time of their wedding in March 1916; he left with his regiment for France three months later. To his great good fortune he had been shipped home from the front within six months – on 8 November 1916, to be precise – suffering, like thousands of others, from trench fever, a debilitating bacterial infection that, essentially, arises from too many people living close together in insanitary conditions. Later an interviewer asked Tolkien if he had written much in the trenches: 'You might scribble something on the back of an envelope and shove it in your back pocket, but that's all,' he replied. 'You'd be crouching down among flies and filth.'[5] Most patients recovered in a matter of weeks. Tolkien's bouts kept recurring, keeping him in England and away from the war. The longevity of the illness must have felt a reprieve, an offer of hope. Edith travelled north from Cheltenham with baby John to join him.

Shortly after the war Edith pointed out – somewhat tartly, perhaps – that, to all intents and purposes, Tolkien had spent the last two years of the conflict in bed, albeit at various locations around Britain.[6] It meant that she had to uproot every few months and find accommodation close to wherever he was stationed. Every time he came close to fitness he would have a relapse. He never actually returned to the front. However, they cannot have known that and, even one year on in Roos, they can hardly have dared to hope for it in the circumstances. Two of Tolkien's three closest friends were already dead: one, Rob Gilson, had been lost in 'no man's land' on the first day of the Battle of the Somme, the other, Geoffrey Bache (G.B.) Smith, had died from complications after being hit by a stray shell behind the lines.

In this context it is hardly surprising that the tale of Beren and Lúthien is a tale of impossible love. The image of his wife dancing in the quiet of the woodland is rescued from convention, from predictability, by the force of the emotion that created it and kept it alive for more than 50 years. It is not purely an image of love, but of love retrieved, beyond hope, from an oceanic feeling of loss, a magical, irrational, senseless survival among the wreckage of a generation.

Perhaps the orphaned Ronald might be expected to have been inured to such loss, or, perhaps, more susceptible. It is hard to imagine that he could not have thought that profound sorrow was an ingrained part of life. The development of his small group of close friends had been vital to Tolkien. He had felt a sense of being a kindred spirit with them, which was not to reappear in his life until the arrival of C.S. Lewis and their creation of the Inklings, a circle of like-minded academics who met regularly in Oxford in the 1930s and 1940s, sometimes to hear Lewis or Tolkien read early drafts of their work aloud.

Tolkien and his three close friends had met when they were all at King Edward's Grammar School in Birmingham. Although they were not of similar tastes or talents, they enjoyed one another's sometimes quirky enthusiasms, interpreting them as a sign of their collective difference. The friendships were formalized into the Tea Club, Barrovian Society (the second part after the Barrow's Stores where they often met), later abbreviated to TCBS. Clearly they indulged a little in self-mythologizing, as adolescents do. Tolkien, for one, compared them to the Pre-Raphaelites. They gave their meetings grandiose titles: one, after they had left school, which took place at the Wandsworth home of the fourth member, Christopher Wiseman, was referred to as the Council of London. Tolkien wrote about their ambitions, their great hopes for themselves, using words like nobility and holiness.[7] You don't have to know much about Tolkien's life or work to know that he was unlikely to use either word lightly. It's hard to think of two qualities he held dearer.

The TCBS inspired hope in Tolkien – perhaps for the first time in his life – and gave him precious confidence in his writing. He was still referring to the deaths of Gilson and Smith as a way of defining the horror of war some 50 years later in his preface to the second edition of *The Lord of the Rings* (1966). It is difficult to read his comments and still to maintain – whatever one thinks of the genre – that Tolkien's writing is escapist: the signals about war and its oppression, about duty and its burdens, are unmistakable.

From what one can see, Tolkien shared with his friends the desire to create a mythology that would do justice to his idea of England. Collectively, they hoped to achieve great things. With two of them dead, Tolkien must have wondered if he would escape the fate of his friends – and millions like them. How, then, could he make their deaths less meaningless? It is more than likely that, if he had remained in France, he would have died, if not before, then with most of his battalion at Chemin des Dames, around the time he was walking with his wife in Roos.[8]

The death of G.B. Smith was a particular blow. Shortly after the war, at the request of Smith's mother, Tolkien ensured that a slim book of Smith's verse was published and contributed a brief introduction to it. It was called *A Spring Harvest*. Its imagery and thought are conventional, but, for all that, rather better than Tolkien's own work of the period. Their work has much in common, however, and several poems seem to prefigure ideas or phrases in *The Lord of the Rings* and other works. A poem called 'Wind over the Sea', for example, which Tolkien in his introduction says could date from as early as 1910, when Smith was 16 (that is, when the two were still at school together) opens with 'the grey heavens'. Its middle section contains a description of a wind racing in from the sea, 'driving the clouds and the breakers before it' and asks the question 'Who are these on the wind, riders and riderless horses?', which recalled to me at least the horses in the flood at the ford of Bruinen. It closes with mention of the 'long straight road', perhaps prefiguring Tolkien's own lost straight road to Tol Eressëa.

There is nothing invidious about this kind of borrowing. You can't read *A Spring Harvest* – something I suspect not many people have ever done – and not be aware of the importance of friendship, and more, of a particular group of friends, to the author, any more than you can avoid the sense of someone trying to work out his experiences with a range of literary devices that are unequal to the task. It makes for an interesting tension in the writing. Behind the sensibility that Smith and Tolkien clearly shared, Smith seems the more willing to articulate a personal vision. Tolkien often appears, even when writing about particularities, to be striving for generalizations, for emblems and signs of emotion, not the thing itself. It's hard to imagine him writing with the directness that, for instance, Smith does:

> Let's have no word of all the sweat and blood.
> Of all the noise and strife and dust and smoke
> (We who have seen Death surging like a flood,
> Wave upon wave, that leaped and raced and broke).

Smith allows death its historic status as an abstraction. The phrase could merely be figurative, rhetorical: except that we know that it wasn't. It was literal, almost an understatement. The convention may dilute the force of the sentiment, but it is also rescued from cliché by the reality of the description.

I thought about Smith again, and the devastation visited on their generation, when I came to visit Tolkien's grave in the municipal cemetery at Wolvercote, on the northern outskirts of Oxford. Not far from the corner where Tolkien lies a funeral was taking place. The Iraq war was at its height and two young men of the family were in uniform, one army and one RAF. Smith's parents lost both their sons in the war. As a parent now I wondered bleakly how all-devouring that kind of grief must be, how, if at all, people could survive it.

Wolvercote is an open and generous place, level and well-tended, surrounded by high hedges blocking out the sight if not the sounds of the adjacent roads. In particular, it is hard to avoid the roar of the Banbury Road behind you to the east, like a none-too-distant jet always on the point on landing. A memorial chapel sits at the cemetery's centre, the hub from which various paths break the plots into different districts loosely dedicated to various religious and ethnic groups – Greeks, Jews, Poles, Catholics, Russians, Yugoslavs – for all the world like a homage to a central European city. There are a few youngish trees, but there is little of the centuries-old charm of the archetypal English churchyard, yew tree standing guard over broken, mossy grave stones, brambles engulfing the forgotten dead.

Wolvercote has in fact won awards. As I entered the gate my attention was subtly drawn to two plaques for the Cemetery of the Year competition by the side of the path. One was for 1999, the other for 2001. A little further on you begin to see ankle-height markers in the neat, trim verge discreetly directing you to Tolkien's grave. He is the only occupant afforded such publicity, modest though it is. Yet, this being Oxford, he is not alone in having some degree of celebrity. The philosopher Isaiah Berlin is here, for instance, under a remarkably ostentatious and imposing slab, as are the biographer and critic Richard Ellman, and the poet Elizabeth Jennings. Jennings, charmingly, has just the single word 'poet' beneath her name. Tolkien, I suspect, would have been just as happy among the less exalted, the Huggins, the Bucklands and the Byngs.

It is some time since I visited a cemetery for anything other than personal reasons, but it was the sort of thing my adolescent self found quite attractive, especially when the cemetery in question, like Highgate, for instance, had a high quota of 'name' residents.

Coming here to Wolvercote was a small act of homage to myself, a little nod of recognition back. Also, even though I already knew what it said, I wanted to see for myself what was written on Tolkien's grave.

Markers aside, Tolkien's grave, which he shares with his wife, is a discreet affair, tucked away democratically in an ordinary row in the Catholic quarter. Given the cult that has attached itself to Tolkien and his work, I feared for the worst, the kind of fate that has befallen Jim Morrison's last resting place in the cemetery of Père Lachaise in Paris, where graffiti, lachrymose outpourings and litter are the order of the day. Here roses flourish on the grave itself, as does an extraordinarily large rosemary bush, which fills the air with sweet, rueful scent each time you brush past. There are letters and postcards here, but they have been neatly collated and folded into a plastic wallet, presumably to protect them from the weather. Perhaps, like the flowers, they are regularly refreshed. It is, of course, a sobering thought that Tolkien might receive fan mail at Wolvercote, but, on the other hand, why not? It seems analogous to Tolkien's own efforts at rewriting some of his work in Anglo-Saxon, not so much an exercise in futility as simply a pointer to the emotional significance of the act.

The Tolkiens' headstone is simply inscribed:
Edith Mary Tolkien, 1889–1971. Lúthien.
John Ronald Reuel Tolkien, 1892–1973. Beren.

The emphatic equation of the Tolkiens' marriage with his central myth of Beren and Lúthien changes the way one thinks about his work. Fantasy and epic romance inevitably operate at several removes from reality, but the creative instincts that underlie them, and the raw materials of emotion and experience, are no different from those that result in the most detailed realism. It is easy to miss in the mythologizing, in the almost absurd breadth and depth of his canvas, but Tolkien's work is as personal as any writer's and perhaps – given its idiosyncrasy – more so than most.

Chapter Three
The temple of Nodens at Lydney Park, Gloucestershire

'I wonder what would happen if they brought the ring back here. Sounds far-fetched, but you never know.' It was the parting shot from Paul, one of a group of men dowsing for water beside the temple, as he turned to follow the path down from the complex and walked out of my field of vision around the curve of the hill. I stayed on the temple steps, looking over the dense woodland towards the silver-grey strip of the Severn Estuary at low tide, some time around noon, the great river holding its breath to reveal thick expanses of mud spreading between the coasts of the West Country and Wales.

Although I was on the northern side of the estuary I was not in fact in Wales, but at Lydney, among the last few acres of England before it cedes to the Celts. I had come here, to Dwarf's Hill, in search of hobbit holes. I hadn't bargained for a ring story, too. It almost seemed too much.

Ultimately what brought me here was the same thing that

brought Tolkien in 1928: a pagan Roman temple. It had been known for some time that the site was something out of the ordinary, certainly since the 18th century, when it and the land around it, which constitute Lydney Park, were bought by the Bathurst family, in whose possession it remains. In the late 1920s Sir Mortimer Wheeler and his wife Tessa, both eminent archaeologists, were commissioned to make a thorough examination of the site. Tolkien was invited here in a professional capacity, being at that point Professor of Anglo-Saxon at Oxford, and stayed on a number of occasions in the main house. He later contributed a chapter to the published report for the Society of Antiquaries[1] on the origin and meaning of the name 'Nodens', the god to whom the temple complex is dedicated and of whom there is little other record, apart from the fact that the smaller of two silver statuettes pulled out of Cockersand Moss, at the mouth of the River Lune in Lancashire, in 1718, bore a dedication to Mars Nodontis. (Whether there was another temple nearby is a matter of conjecture. None has been found and the statuettes have in any case since disappeared.)

Tolkien found a web of meanings and associations that stretched across a wide range of early northern European languages, but the Wheelers' discoveries need to be examined first. The site they were working on expands over five flat acres on the top of Dwarf's Hill – the historic, Anglo-Saxon, rather than contemporary name for it, I admit, since today it is known as Camp Hill. Mortimer Wheeler was fond enough of the ancient name, which survived long into the second millennium, to use it in his report. The hill stands some 200 feet above sea level, sandwiched between the

River Severn to the south and the Forest of Dean to the north. As far as is known, it was first occupied in the first century BC, as evidenced by the remains of a hill-fort, as well as by the innumerable shallow iron works dug, unusually, into the side of the hill, many of which are still visible to this day. Although it would be misleading to call these mine shafts, they are clearly of a different order from the open-cast mining that typified Iron Age attempts to retrieve the precious ore, the remains of which are known as 'scowls' locally. (If I could find a way of linking this to Tolkien's word 'smials' with even a little decency, I would.)

Romans – or Romano-Britons – occupied the site some time during the second or third centuries AD and continued to mine the rich hill. One such mine, sited towards the north of the complex, extends some 50 feet into the ground; it and the other Roman mines here are the only ones extant in Britain. The temple itself dates from around 364–7. It must have had a relatively brief heyday, since Rome withdrew its legions from England in 410. Although coins, for instance, have been found from the fifth century, the late fourth century saw a defensive wall built around the precinct, and the strengthening of the Iron Age banks and ditches. Evidence of habitation dwindles after that, and the site seems to have been eventually abandoned. Whether that was because it became unsustainable, or because it was attacked by the Saxons, is open to question. There is suggestion of a fire, which might make the latter seem more likely, although Wheeler thought it simply fell into disuse.

Tolkien's chapter, published in 1932 and not reprinted since (to my knowledge), is an extraordinary testament to his skill and erudition. In just over five densely argued pages he runs through the known mythical figures whom he could plausibly associate with Nodens, including Lear and Lludd, and analyses the name itself in merciless detail to extract every last drop of meaning: it is as if he is struggling to recreate a desert from a single grain of sand. The degree of learning on display is astonishing. One paragraph runs through seven languages – Gothic, Old English, Old Saxon, Old High German, Old Norse, Lithuanian and Lettish (Latvian) – in search of an unrecorded but hypothesized Germanic root verb. Elsewhere he reaches back through vowel shifts – the way the pronunciations of words change when they are grafted onto one language from another – from the very distant to the prehistoric Indo-European family of tongues, feeling his way through to a source that might make sense of the evidence. Tolkien's conclusion is that Nodens is – or was – a snarer, catcher or hunter of some description. But he cannot – or does not – go further and explain what that implies. It ties in with a number of votive offerings found at Lydney, which are in the shape of dogs. He does note an echo of one analogous figure in Celtic myth, Núada Argat-lam – Núada of the silver hand – a king whose power is bound up in the hand itself.

It is Tolkien's linguistic approach and technique that are most illuminating, the extent to which legend and language are used as mutually supportive tools in a bid to rescue meaning – and, behind that, the cultural legacy of a forgotten people – from the last remaining scraps of information left to us. This is not simply about the beliefs of those who built the temple and who worshipped here. It is about the ancestry of the gods and the cultures they graced, the legends they inhabited before the arrival of the Romans to assimilate or destroy them, before even the arrival of the Celtic tribes from mainland Europe, arguably as much as 1,500 years earlier, when Nodens already served a remote and unknown people, whose monuments, mere stones, inspire both dread and awe.

It is a commonplace argument in critiques of Tolkien's work that one of the great strengths of *The Lord of the Rings* is the depth or, if you prefer, the illusion of depth provided by the background histories, the heroic – mostly tragic – tales of the First and Second Ages, which Tolkien had in fact written first and which are referred to throughout. It was something that he was aware of himself and that made him wonder whether publication of *The Silmarillion* would be a mistake.[2]

Yet it is not just the fall of Gondolin or the battles of Isildur and Elendil that contribute to that effect. It is also that sense of lost histories, of peoples whose very names have already been obliterated, or to whom the victories and defeats in the west are largely an irrelevance that, either way, will spell a wider kind of defeat.

I am thinking in particular of the makers of the Púkel men, great primitive stone figures, their features all but erased save for the holes that were their eyes, who move Merry, seeing them for the first time as he rides with the men of Rohan, to a kind of sorrow. Nothing is known of them: they have no tales and no songs; they have no name. Their only memorials are Dunharrow and the stone men they made to guard its road in the dark pre-history of Middle Earth.[3]

They stand to Rohan as builders of Stonehenge or Wayland's

Smithy do to us. It is a peculiarly Tolkienish sentiment, this, the capacity to be profoundly moved by the idea of the distant, unknown, entirely lost past.[4] Some might characterize Tolkien's world, as Jonathan Miller has done, as being one of 'remote, meaningless antiquity',[5] but that misses the point of Tolkien's life's work, which was precisely to restore to antiquity its meanings and identities. In Dunharrow – and later too in a different way with Ghan-buri-Ghan and the woses, the wild men of the woods – we see Tolkien making room within his work to articulate the very emotion that drove him to create it in the first place. Among other purposes, it serves to project the reader further into that created world, more aware of the layers of history and culture that underlie it, wondering more about its dark periphery, sharing Merry's pity.

Tolkien's work on Nodens was just such an act of rescue or recovery. The site as a whole is a kind of microcosm of the lost England of his heart. If nothing else, its iron ore ensured that the area would attract attention and settlement. Lydney saw a succession of peoples struggling to escape oblivion, to escape the fate of those who, in Milton's phrase, are 'blotted out and rased from the books of life'. Simply, they were struggling to survive, fending off their own erasure while assuming into their own cultures and languages such traces of the defeated as they found valuable or expedient. There are in fact the ruins of a Norman castle on the adjacent hill – now known as Little Camp Hill – which has yet to be properly excavated. It is a reminder of the loss that sorrowed Tolkien most of all, that of the Anglo-Saxon language and culture that thrived in the centuries before 1066. The Normans, for good or ill, provided a stability to England, a continuity that has yet, really, to be broken. Their stamp is on the last 1,000 years of English history, where the 2,000 previous to their arrival is a tangle of invasions – which, for whatever reason, the inhabitants of the islands seem to have been incapable of repelling – followed by assimilation before the next wave of migrants appeared off the eastern coasts.

It is hard, for me at least, to think of England, this cramped little country, or of any other part of the island of Great Britain in terms of tribes or kingdoms, let alone the cantons that comprised the country under the 400-odd years of Roman occupation. It is easy to forget in today's relative homogeneity that it was not always so and that even the later small Anglo-Saxon kingdoms, such as Mercia and Wessex, represented the agglomeration of many yet smaller tribal groups under an imported, even alien political structure. Lydney, however, seems always to have been liminal. In his article Tolkien refers to Nodens of the Silures, but actually the site was – much as it is now – on the border, with the wild Silures to the west and north, and the Dobunni to the east. The Silures resisted the encroachment of Rome, sheltering Caractacus after his abortive attempt to repel the invading legions in Kent. However, they were essentially a pastoral people and they have left no buildings behind them. The Dobunni territory fits very closely to that of the later West Mercia: if Lydney marks its borders in the west, then Wood Eaton – interestingly Tolkien's first choice of name for Buckland – which is on the River Cherwell to the north of Oxford, marks it in the east.

I found myself in Lydney at the invitation of Sylvia Jones, the curator of Lydney Park. Since the house and gardens are open to the public for only 30 days each year, the last of those in May, I was fortunate that Sylvia was willing to offer me access. More than that, she generously devoted a couple of hours to showing me round the site herself and answering my no doubt unoriginal questions.

The park has been in the Bathurst family since 1719, although the current house, in which Tolkien would have stayed when he visited the archaeological dig, dates from 1875. The family acquired a peerage, the viscountcy of Bledisloe, in 1935, by way of thanks for the then head of the family's service as Governor General of New Zealand. Having been Governor General, Viscount Bledisloe spent some time encouraging local families to emigrate to New Zealand: members of one such family ended up winning Oscars for work on the film of *The Lord of the Rings*. With the ubiquity of the National Trust and English Heritage these days, one sometimes forget how many great houses and gardens are still in private hands. Lydney Park is one such example.

The estate sits just to the north of the main Gloucester–Chepstow road, a dozen or so miles east of the Severn Bridge. Sylvia met me at the entrance to the house, first showing me the small museum, which has a number of artefacts from the Roman excavations, among other things, although nothing like the more than 8,000 items that have actually been dug up over the years. I must admit I felt somewhat nervous. It wasn't just the social pressure, the slight self-conscious embarrassment of having a personal tour of the site. It was also a volatile mix of excitement and doubt arising from the phone conversation we had had to arrange the visit. There was the Nodens connection, yes, but there were also these holes in the hillside associated in local folklore with 'little people'. A source for hobbits and hobbit holes? I wasn't sure she couldn't hear surges of disbelief and wonder in my voice as I confirmed our meeting.

I have been around the Tolkien industry – never mind the Tolkien obsessives – long enough to know that everyone has their own dearly held and frequently sacrosanct theories about his sources of inspiration for particular passages or places. I'm not saying that I'm immune to this, but I'm enough of a cynic to think that usually the truth is the other way around: people are reminded of the books when they see particular things.

Since I've been writing this book I've become yet more wary, having been cornered by enough eager fans concerned to persuade me that the B7623 or similar is surely the true model for the East Road through the Shire – when there's no evidence that Tolkien ever came within a hundred miles of it, let alone lifted its route for his life's work – to last me a lifetime. A good example of this tendency appears in a response to an article by Professor David Hinton (discussed in Chapter 8) on the charter boundary marks of the Berkshire Downs and their influence on Tolkien.[6] The article drew forth from a correspondent, Fred Mustill, the claim that:

> After a visit to Kinver Edge in Worcestershire, there is little doubt in my mind where Tolkien got his inspiration for hobbit holes. There are numerous dry and well-drained dwellings there, hewn into the soft sandstone cliffs. They are nothing like Saxon sunken-floored dwellings…but are true subterranean houses with large

doors, windows, and chimneys. In fact, they are just as Tolkien described hobbit holes. There are even pine trees there, just as in Tolkien's drawings of Hobbiton.

I have no problem with Kinver Edge – it's a fascinating and mysterious place – but there is simply nothing to connect it to Tolkien.

As you can imagine, hearing Sylvia say that she could show me Tolkien's inspiration for hobbit holes fired some contradictory feelings in me. After all, Tolkien himself said that the root of *The Hobbit* – and therefore of *The Lord of the Rings* – was in the idea of a hole in which a hobbit lived, which sprang into his mind unbidden when he really should have been marking examination papers. He claimed that at that point he certainly didn't know himself what hobbits were, or why they should live in holes in the ground in the first place. A source for that single idea, from which his greatest success grew, must also in some respects be the ultimate source for both *The Lord of the Rings* and *The Hobbit*, since without that seed there would have been nothing. When he wrote *The Hobbit* he had little intention of linking it to *The Silmarillion* – which he adored – and, clearly, if he had not written *The Hobbit* it seems extremely unlikely that *The Lord of the Rings* would ever even have been started.

Despite my misgivings, therefore, I was extremely curious about what might lie ahead. Travelling down, I had mostly been preoccupied with the kind of holes I would be presented with and just how seriously to take them, amusing myself with how little they were likely to have in common with the prosperous Edwardianism of those that we see the insides of in the Shire – most notably, of course, Bag End, Bilbo and Frodo's bourgeois home.

I can't explain how, but I had also presumed or persuaded myself that the site would be flat, maybe even some kind of moorland. Perhaps that is simply the kind of landscape that I associate with Roman Britain, thanks to some long forgotten scrap of 1970s educational television, or maybe a Ladybird book about Julius Caesar or Boadicea. What I wasn't prepared for, of course, was the reality.

The house at Lydney Park is a substantial late Victorian affair, unostentatious despite its size. The way the long private drive snakes up from the main road reminded me a little of the approach to San Simeon, William Randolph Hearst's quixotic fantasy castle outside San Obispo on the coast of California. That this is on a smaller scale is hardly to its detriment: most of the palaces of Europe are on a smaller scale than that. Maybe the connection was also about the sense of anticipation that such driveways arouse. I expected to see an imposing pile sitting imperiously at the end of the drive. Instead the house sits off to one side, almost casual and certainly informal, less an expression of power and wealth than simply somewhere elegant and spacious to live.

From the house Sylvia led me down through a wide iron gate into a steep, heavily wooded valley gouged between the two hills – Camp Hill straight ahead and Little Camp Hill, which to my mind was not appreciably smaller, to the left. A thin brown stream slipped almost unnoticed through the thick grass on the valley floor. As we walked she told me a little of the history of the area. A mile or so south is the River Severn, one of the great tidal rivers of England, on which the mercantile wealth of Bristol was built, its ships spreading west to the Americas and elsewhere. In Roman times, however, the river was wider and came right up into the valley we were crossing. A little further down, where the stream curves out of sight, hugging close to Little Camp Hill, Roman cobblestones belonging to a harbour, or at least its remains, have been found. The temple clearly had strong associations with the sea: the floor was originally graced with a frieze of sea monsters and fish. Investigators have also dug up an illustration of a boy angling, dated to the first century AD and thus one of the earliest known examples of such an image – and perhaps, too, of the technique itself. This is one of those places where artefacts seem almost embarrassing in their abundance.

We were now in the deer park, where three herds of fallow deer roam freely, if nervously. I saw an auburn-coated doe, a fallow I think, start, perhaps at our presence, and flit away into the soft, broken shadows of the trees, as if in some ancestral memory of a great hunt. She could have come from a medieval tableau or a romance such as *Sir Gawain and the Green Knight*. Sylvia tells me of evidence that Simon de Montfort, the 13th-century nobleman and founder of the English Parliament, once stayed in the now-ruined Norman castle. Why Little Camp Hill hasn't yet been formally excavated I don't know: it seems a strange opportunity to pass up. I suspect that Tolkien might have felt, as I do, that the past is so difficult to know – the survival of anything from it so arbitrary and precious – that any chance to rescue the merest fragment of it from oblivion should not be given up lightly.

The gradient on Camp Hill is pretty sharp. As I looked back across the valley to the house, now trivial in the distance, and the sheep flecking the fields like so many spots of rain, I wondered what it must have been like for the Romans to climb the hill, or more likely to be carried, and to feel that lovely sense of being raised out of your troubles, slowly lifting you above quotidian things. I thought of Les Murray's poem 'Quintets for Robert Morley', which argues that it is the fat men of history, those with the time and inclination to lounge around, with the wealth to afford palanquins or litters, who have bequeathed us civilization. I wondered whether coming to the temple here carried with it a sense of safety or a sense of risk. For all that the Britons had been pacified, still this was the very margin of the empire, always fraught, a restless peace being maintained with the Silures a mile of two to the west and the real power of Rome a long way behind you, nearer the centre of the known world. This was a pagan temple, too, when the empire had already turned Christian, and one dedicated to a Celtic god at that. Yet Sylvia replied, in answer to my question, that people came from across the empire to worship here.

The old entrance to the temple is on your right as you near the summit of the hill, announced now by no more than a grassy knoll, but shaped, I thought, like a snake's tongue, the V formed by the spaces where two sets of steps would have taken you up. Just past this point Sylvia darted off into what appeared to be undergrowth and stopped. She gestured towards what looked like an uninviting clump of ferns – especially uninviting as I now had snakes on my mind. Still, it was what I had come to see and she stood back with a hint of almost parental pride to let me get a closer look. I followed her cautiously down the slope, feeling as much as anything that I needed at the very least to make a show of being overwhelmed with excitement, whatever was down there and whatever my real emotions on the subject. It seemed the polite thing to do.

I was struggling desperately to come up with something interesting to say, or even something insightful to ask. Unfortunately, I could do little more than repeat the words 'Fantastic' and 'Great' at regular intervals. It is one of the old Iron Age mineheads, a stone crossbeam supported by two verticals, two feet high and some four feet wide, and quite square and regular. The doorway itself is at a 90-degree angle to the hill, set at the bottom of a small gulley and so protected from any winds. I slid down the reddish earth to the opening, itself sheltered by a pine tree, almost fallen, reaching out horizontally from the hillside by the path, maybe six or eight feet above. I squatted down, eyeing the lintel nervously. It seemed solid enough. I felt as if Sylvia, standing a few feet away, was watching me closely, looking for evidence that I was suitably impressed. I looked inside. The hole had been burrowed into the dark rocky heart of the hill, but not far, perhaps only a few feet. I could probably have lain in it, although I didn't feel especially disposed to do so. It felt a little like an empty burial chamber. I wondered how long I should sit there on my haunches, staring intently into the dark interior, before it would be polite to move on.

It is not that I wasn't impressed, simply that I didn't quite know what to think. It is hard, after all, when faced with something like this, to know what connections to make, or at least what connections might be valid. For one thing, my natural cynicism is hard to override. I think I was hoping for some kind of judgemental epiphany, an unarguable insight into the truth or otherwise of the claim. All I felt was ambivalence, the competing tugs of doubt and hope on my affections. The hole was clearly 'made' and in no way natural, but still ... I demurred as graciously as I could, deciding to defer a final decision for myself till later.

Sylvia told me that there are dozens of holes like it all over the hill, most of which she discourages people from visiting simply because they are unsafe. When Tolkien came here, she added, he was very interested in the folklore that surrounded Dwarf's Hill. The very name derives from strange local stories about little people living in these holes. I was tempted to connect these little people of local folklore with the discovery some time ago, inside one of the Roman-period miners' huts, of a miniature pickaxe, which presumably was some kind of votive offering to Nodens.

In the meantime Sylvia led me up to the temple. The path curves around the crest of the hill and we could hear voices, men's voices, before we could see anyone. I already knew who they were. They were dowsers, there at Sylvia's invitation to try to find the water source for the temple baths. Truth be told, I was none too keen to meet them. Partly, of course, this was pure selfish greed: I wanted the site to myself. But there was another kind of aversion at play too. I am enough a child of the 1970s to instantly associate dowsing with raddled old hippies: wispy beards, woolly hats, dogs on string, jazz cigarettes. I remember it being a staple of interviews in the music paper the *NME* that bands would be constantly going off to 'get their heads together' in the country, tuning in to the ley lines and so on. Naturally I expected to find either a bunch of late 40-something men in faded Gentle Giant t-shirts milling about the place.

If I had been more observant I'd probably have noticed the E-series silver Mercedes parked at the base of the hill. Yet I don't know if even then I'd have made the connection with dowsing. It is, quite clearly, a rather more lucrative line of business than I had realized. The dowsers themselves were, thankfully, quite normal. There were six of them. They gave the impression of being prosperous folk who had taken up dowsing after retirement, the way other people take up religion or golf. It turned out that they also do a spot of metal-detecting on the side.

Sylvia introduced me to them, but I didn't catch all their names. Two of them came over to show her something they'd found. There was some dispute over what it was. Max thought it was a figure of a deer. Sylvia pushed strongly for its being a human hand, albeit a broken one. She seemed to feel quite proprietorial about it, but it would make sense. The temple clearly functioned, in part, as a place of healing and there have been numerous finds of votive offerings in the shape of particular body parts, among them hands. Out of courtesy they showed the object to me. It just looked a shapeless mass, but that didn't seem a particularly constructive comment to make. I would have liked it to be a hand, of course, to tie it in with Núada Argat-lam, but I couldn't really convince myself of anything. Glyn sidled up to me and said, *sotto voce*, that it was just as likely to be a rabbit. The disagreement fizzled on.

In any case, I was more interested in looking at the site itself. As we came out onto the levelled peak of the hill it had been immediately apparent that this was something out of the ordinary. There are four buildings in the temple complex: the temple itself, the dormitory, the baths and the guest house. The last of these – also the largest of the four – is not currently visible, since the present Lord Bledisloe likes to hold shooting parties up here and therefore maintains it waist-deep in ferns to accommodate the game.

The hill-top is largely bare otherwise, with panoramic views down the Severn to the south and west, although to the north, where the banks and ditches of the remaining Iron Age earthworks are to be found, it is more heavily wooded. It had failed to occur to me when we were walking up the hill, but it must have been an obvious choice for the pre-Roman hill-fort: steep slopes and clear sight-lines for miles around. It is an obvious site for worship, too, removed, elevated and – just on the basis of its position – blessed with the kind of good fortune that one would want a god to have. Even though what remains are left of the Roman buildings are now no more than a couple of feet high, at best, and mostly less, the extent of its survival is still almost shocking. I think what is so surprising is that the site hasn't been adapted to any other use in the intervening centuries, or adopted by another people and buried beneath their own buildings. As a result, for all the decay in evidence, it is nonetheless easy to imagine the complex as the Romans knew it.

I must admit to having been taken aback by the sophistication of what can be seen there. Insofar as I had ever considered Roman temples before, I would have expected them to be given over to devotion to the godhead, to be, not necessarily ascetic, but still dedicated to the divine. The presence of a substantial guest house here somewhat disrupts that prejudice. It may not quite have been a hotel, but it was not too far removed from one. Paganism too – clearly wrongly – connotes for me a kind of primitivism wholly at odds with the way it is synthesized at Lydney into what, in another context, we might call bourgeois society. Part of what is called the 'dormitory' – not for sleeping in but for seeking holy inspiration in dreams – may also have been some kind of retail outlet for offerings to the temple. We can only speculate as to the motives that led a wealthy Roman to make the journey here: whether the attraction was a profound, spiritual one, whether it signified some kind of regret for a lost heritage, or whether it merely provided a superficial thrill, the frisson of difference, for more jaded cultural appetites. But it seems clear that those who came – certainly when the site was at its zenith – felt that Lydney was a place of safety, despite its location on the very margins of the empire. Such a sense of security – even if touched with complacency – is a measure of the Romans' success in pacifying their enemies, whether by formally conquering them or simply by intimidating them into quiescence. Lydney, for all its Celtic roots, was thoroughly Romanized. The presence of such buildings – I hesitate to use the phrase but it feels almost as if it had been a kind of leisure complex – in the middle of what had previously been an Iron Age fortification illustrates the acute differences in power and security felt by the Romans and Celts, the one people self-assured, the other vulnerable and wary.

Even for the Romans, however, there were things in the world to be feared aside from potential enemies. At its peak there were probably some 300 people living at Lydney. Whatever it had to offer spiritually, it was always also a physical sanctuary from the wilderness below. It is easy to forget in England, where the countryside – the very word indicating that nature has been tamed – has had all its danger drained for centuries, that well into recorded history there have been wild places that contained very real dangers for anyone. In Roman times the woods surrounding Lydney, which still bleed into the closed world of the Forest of Dean to the north, were full of wolves, bears and wild boars. One of the tablets found at the site records the gratitude of a young boy to the god for a lucky escape.

The Forest of Dean held other risks too. Given that one of Tolkien's primary interests was in the points at which language and myth enter the historical record, I thought it made sense to go back, as part of my research, to the first entrance of the idea of England as a place whose physical and cultural identity was worthy of delineation. For me that meant going back to the Elizabethan antiquary William Camden, whose *Britannia,* published in 1586, is arguably the first serious historical work to capture and celebrate the emergent British nations. Camden travelled the length and breadth of the island, recording its cities and towns, its ancient monuments and Roman ruins, its folklore and its landscapes. There had been other such books, most obviously Leland's *Itinerary,* written in the 1530s, but none as thorough or rich as Camden's. Writing of the Forest of Dean Camden says that it was:

> a wonderful, thick forest, and in former times dark and terrible, by reason of crooked and winding ways, as also the grisly shade therein, that it made the inhabitants more fierce and bolder to commit robberies.

One can only imagine how much more danger it can have held a thousand years previously.

If we are inclined to forget how dark and bloody the English valleys and wealds once were, then the converse is true too: we too often fail to remember that there are hardly any English landscapes that one can really believe are in any sense 'natural'. Almost all have been reshaped and moulded to the interests of human beings, whether through agriculture or land clearance or through the introduction of new species. At Lydney, for instance, aside from the level hill-top there is the matter of Plane Tree Valley, which lies below Camp Hill, the trees in which are descended from those first imported by the Romans themselves.

By this time the beeping of the metal detectors was beginning to get irksome. Sylvia led me on to the dormitory and the bathhouse. The conduit between the water tank and the bath is now a badger's sett. The tank itself is empty and the dowsers are here to try to find its water source, without much success. Beyond that there is a tangle of trees and the Iron Age defences. Sylvia and I said our goodbyes; she kindly added that I was free to stay as long as I liked.

I wandered off towards the trees, hoping to buy some time so that the dowsers would leave and I would have the place to myself. I sat at the base of an oak tree, its roots folding over themselves like tumbling water, and watched the game birds teeming in the ferns. I wrote some notes, but dark clouds seemed to be massing in the sky. The weather hadn't been better than mixed all day and I didn't really want to get caught up here in a storm. Reluctantly I headed off, still trying to work out what I thought about the hobbit hole. Could it really have been the spark that ignited Tolkien's imagination?

As I approached the temple again, I could see that the dowsers were also preparing to leave. One of them, a tallish, slender man named Paul, came up to me and asked if I'd like to try my hand at dowsing. Actually I didn't particularly, but not having done it before – and being fairly sceptical anyway – I agreed to try it. Paul volunteered that he had thought that dowsing was nonsense, too, but he used to own a golf-course and, much to his surprise, dowsing had proved to be the only reliable way of identifying water beneath the ground. He also said that they had finally found water at Lydney. The reason it had taken so long was that the water wasn't where it ought to be, that is, adjacent to the tank. It was in an unhelpful if interesting place: the source bisected the temple perfectly from the southeast corner to the northwest, before heading for the baths. The likelihood of their being allowed to dig it up, given where it was, was minimal.

Paul handed me his dowsing rods, two single sections of wire looking for all the world like coat-hangers bent at right angles. The shorter, vertical section of each was encased in a narrow wooden tubular grip, not much thicker than a cigarette. I paced slowly across the temple, feeling slightly foolish, but, just as Paul had said, there was a band across the centre, maybe three feet across, where the rods went wild, swinging violently outwards like the antennae of some great slow insect. Apparently for most people they swing inwards: I have no idea what this means. I did it a couple of times and got the same response. My worldview shifted uneasily.

We talked a little about what I was doing. Paul knew the films based on *The Lord of the Rings*, of course, but I am not sure that he knew the book. His friends had already left by then and he was packing up to go. Then he mentioned the ring. I had known nothing about this until Sylvia had sprung it on me, almost in passing, as we stood in the museum. The story is this. One of the artefacts attached to the temple at Lydney is a curse tablet, an invocation for revenge. It reads:

> To the God Nodens. Silvanus has lost a ring. He has [vowed] half its value to Nodens. Among all who bear the name of Senicianus, refuse thou to grant health to exist, until he bring back the ring to the Temple of Nodens.

As curses go this seems extreme, but then it was not uncommon for people to keep much of their wealth in jewellery like this, so it may have meant rather more to Silvanus than the loss of a beloved trinket. It seems extraordinary, but his ring has been found. Not here at Lydney Park, however: it was dug up in a church in Silchester, which is now in Hampshire, in 1785. Senicianus clearly had a new inscription placed on it: '*Seniciane vivas in deo*' ('Senicianus, may you live in the god'). Its home these days is the Vyne Museum at Basingstoke. Taking its lead from Senicianus, the Vyne has declined to return it to Lydney Park.

I think that there is still a vestigial power in the idea of curses, or, more particularly, the idea of invoking a god to enforce a curse, which we can feel despite any general disbelief. It is an act out of the remote past, almost but not quite unintelligible: something we can recognize and would seek to avoid. It is not what people turn to religion for nowadays. In the Christian world, at least, they tend to look to God for mercy rather than wrath. The circularity of this curse in particular, with the restitution of property being subordinate to the ring being returned to the place where the curse was laid, adds to its resonance, emphasizing that the acts enmeshed in the story are reciprocal, mutually responsive. That is why Paul's comment about returning the ring to Lydney seems right: it is not about restoring it to the owner, or some notional proxy of the owner; it is about acknowledging the authority of the god. It would be like disturbing the pattern of history, particularly since the ring has been lost to Nodens and rededicated to the Christian God, which to me is as telling a symbol as any of a period in which belief systems and cultures were in flux, even at war. As Mortimer Wheeler says of the temple builders:

> In the fourth century the darkness was already closing rapidly upon them… The Lydney temple, with its partially transmuted pagan forms, represents the ultimate achievement of some one of these lost rivals to Christianity.[7]

That it was Senicianus, it seems, who picked the winning side makes the apparent failure of Silvanus's curse – to the extent that the ring was never returned – doubly sad. This was a personal loss, but also, in a wider sense, a loss for a pagan culture that is now barely known to us, heard only in the echo of place names, in small things dredged out of the earth.

Clearly, it is a long way from this to the magic ring – not yet even a Ring of Power – that Bilbo wins in the darkness under the mountain in *The Hobbit*. I don't think we can say any more than that the story of Silvanus's ring, which Tolkien must certainly have known, may have caught his imagination and been buried away somewhere in his unconscious. A ring is an unusual device, after all, once you discount the train of thought associated with Richard Wagner, which Tolkien did, and vehemently.[8] What we have here is a ring that bears a curse, that has a more than material significance and that needs to be returned to the place of the curse's making if that curse is to be lifted. We can't make a definite causal link – and Middle Earth would be much duller if we could – but the parallels are certainly thought-provoking.

Standing on the temple steps again, I watched the slow, heavy clouds, gun-metal grey, pass overhead, flashes of sunlight breaking through to light up the glassy water still threading through the estuary. I was there at the wrong time of year, but this must be a superb vantage point to watch the Severn Bore, a surge wave caused by particularly high tides being forced up the narrowing mouth of the estuary, which shrinks from five miles wide to less than a hundred yards as it travels east; at Lydney it is about a mile across. The wave itself, meanwhile, can be up to three metres high. It can in fact be surfed, if you're so inclined. I thought about Tolkien's recurring dream of Atlantis, of the tall wave falling on the green fields and woodlands. I thought too of the meaning of the name 'Lydney'. I had already looked it up in the *Oxford Dictionary of English Place Names*. It had meant 'Lida's island', which, given that in Old English *lida* meant 'sailor', could mean 'the sailor's island'. It sounds Tolkienish enough, with echoes of both Numenor and Tol Eressëa. The trouble is that if you spend long enough with a book like that, pretty much every meaning seems to be suggestive of Middle Earth. In a twisted way this is a tribute to the care that Tolkien lavished on his nomenclature. It does, however, fail to illuminate much in this instance.

Does Roman Britain, I wondered, have any meaning for Middle Earth? In some respects it seems to offer a discontinuity between the groups in which Tolkien was really interested: the Bronze Age settlers and the Celts on one side, and the Angles, Saxons, Jutes, Danes and Swedes, among others, who came later. Rome left its mark on England, certainly, most notably in the founding of so many of our towns and cities, but none at all on the language. I don't have a clear answer to the question. Yet I wonder if we can see the shadow of the Romans at Lydney, especially of those years after 410 when the imperial power withdrew, in two places in *The Lord of the Rings*. The first is in the figures of the Rangers, who are in a kind of exile from their true kingdom in the south, fighting a desperate local battle against the rising darkness. The second is in Gondor itself, or more precisely in its ruined outposts, such as Osgiliath, as much as those it has lost, such as Minas Ithil. Tolkien did heavily imply some kind of equation between Rome and Gondor in a letter of 1967. He explained to his correspondent that Hobbiton and Rivendell are expressly situated on the same latitude as Oxford. It followed, he added, that Minas Tirith is in an equivalent position to Florence and that the victory of Gondor therefore in some respects echoes a renascent Holy Roman Empire.[9]

It seemed worthwhile to take a second look at the alleged hobbit hole I'd been shown. As I came back down the hill on my own there seemed something comfortable about its situation beneath a bent tree below the temple entrance – perhaps simply because I knew it was there now. I sat in the dark doorway of the hole and looked up at the sky through the rippling net of the leaves on the trees. I asked myself how much disbelief it was necessary to suspend to think that this could be Tolkien's source. The answer was, almost to my surprise, not much. He was certainly here, on site, on several occasions in the late 1920s. It's hard to credit that he wouldn't have found or been shown some of the old mineshafts, or heard some of the stories attached to them regarding the 'little people' and the like. I have tried to verify these since, with no success. But of course this is folklore and, to borrow a phrase from another context, absence of evidence can hardly be taken for evidence of absence. Clearly, too, Tolkien transformed what he found, consciously or otherwise, so what's here bears no direct relation to Bag End – although it's fair to ask what would, aside from an Edwardian villa. Can we regard these as proto-hobbit holes? It may be a credulous judgement, but yes, I think we can.

Chapter Four
The Lizard Peninsula, Cornwall

By the time Tolkien reached Roos he had already begun his *Book of Lost Tales*, the earliest of which is a version of the 'Fall of Gondolin' written at Great Haywood in Staffordshire early in 1917, towards the beginning of his convalescence. For all that some of his tastes and talents tended toward the conventional, others certainly did not.

Unlike most of his contemporaries, for instance, Tolkien already had a healthy interest in, and an increasingly detailed knowledge of, obliterated peoples. Specifically, he was fascinated intellectually and entranced emotionally by the way that the Anglo-Saxon peoples of England, and more importantly their language and culture, had been drowned by the Norman Conquest and the succeeding centuries of French cultural domination that came in its wake. In some ways this must have been quite a modish position. An interest in, and celebration of, the 'primitive' cultures underlying sophisticated modernity was prevalent in the early 20th century, developing out of the nationalism of the late 19th century as people sought to find roots for their cultures in folklore and myth. After all, Ezra Pound, still reasonably sane at this point and without doubt something of a modernist avatar, had translated the Anglo-Saxon poem *The Seafarer* in 1911. It is not something you could imagine Tennyson doing: the literature of pre-Norman Conquest England was simply invisible in our culture until the 19th century. Even *Beowulf* remained untranslated into a modern European language until 1820, and then it first appeared in Danish. Importantly, however, Tolkien was developing an interest in what lay behind some of the more intractable problems of understanding – and then translating – a language that had been all but extinguished a thousand years before.

Many people who come to Cornwall feel some kind of artistic stirring, an ill-defined sense of longing anchored in the wild sea and the brilliant light, which has the same watery clarity as that to be found in the South of France. It can make the most mundane of objects seem almost numinous, lit from within. However, most of us do not then go away and spend 60 years creating a cycle of myths. Yet it's not too much of an exaggeration to say that that's what Tolkien did.

Tolkien holidayed on the Lizard in the summer of 1914, staying with Father Vincent Reade from the Birmingham Oratory (Ronald and Edith were only betrothed at this point). The two men roamed widely together and Tolkien seems to have found the experience a catalyst for what became his life's work. With hindsight we tend to assume that everything that summer, made golden now by nostalgia for the vanished worlds of Victorian and Edwardian England, happened under the shadow of war. But there is no particular reason to suppose that this was true of

Tolkien, still less that he could have foreseen the carnage that followed and the personal griefs he was to suffer. What we do know is that his time in Cornwall inspired 'The Voyage of Éarendel, the Evening Star', the first poem, indeed the first writing of any kind, to form a part of his legendarium, although it was actually written in September 1914 at Phoenix Farm in Gedling, Nottinghamshire, then being run by his aunt Jane, the one member of his extended family to whom he remained extremely close all his life. The farm has since been demolished. (I think it's a fair supposition that the Phoenix Farm Car Centre on Arnold Lane and the nearby Phoenix Avenue give a fair approximation of its site, if anyone is interested. Gedling, itself, in 1914 a village well to the east of Nottingham, has now been consumed by the city, much as 20th-century Birmingham has claimed Sarehole.)

The poem is a small beginning for such a vast enterprise. It is about a mariner who sets sail from the west, specifically from 'Westernesse' – an obscure term that Tolkien took from Middle English – and ultimately leaves the confines of the Earth to sail among the stars. Aside from the person of Éarendil (Tolkien later changed the spelling) there is little to indicate what was to come in Middle Earth. It is just a spark. According to Carpenter, when one of Tolkien's close friends, G.B. Smith (see Chapter 2), read the poem he asked what it meant. Tolkien replied that he didn't really know. It could be argued that he spent the rest of his life trying to find out. Éarendil became a fixed point throughout his work, the details of his ascension to the stars modifying as the mythic structure took root. He finds a place in *The Lord of the Rings*, for instance, as an already legendary character from the remote past, in Bilbo's song at Rivendell; and it is the thought of the Silmaril rescued by Beren from Morgoth's Iron Crown, and carried now by Earendil in the night sky, the light of which Galadriel captured in the phial she gave to Frodo, that sustains Sam on the stairs of Cirith Ungol.

Tolkien had been thinking about Éarendil for some months, perhaps since the previous autumn, having come across the following lines in the Anglo Saxon poem *Crist*: '*Éalá! éarendel engla beorhtast ofer middangeard monnum sended*' ('Hail, Éarendel, brightest of angels, above the Middle Earth sent unto men'). In the context of *Crist* they are spoken by the prophets tormented in Hell before the coming of Christ to redeem them. But Tolkien discovered that Earendel had associations in Germanic mythology with both the sea and the stars, and that the lines also echo a Latin prayer pleading for Christ's intercession.[1] His insight, however, was that, just as in philology you could reconstruct words or languages by painstaking comparison with cognate languages, so too you could for myths. Perhaps he could reconstruct the myth that lay behind Éarendel, that one alien, already archaic word in *Crist*. It's a moment that he dramatizes in his unfinished time-travel novel of the 1940s, *The Notion Club Papers*, in which one character, discussing the lines from *Crist* quoted above, describes the excitement, the physical pleasure he experienced discovering the word in a dictionary and sensing a remote and powerful beauty to it, alluring yet unknowable.[2]

In fact, you can see an example of Tolkien's accretive method in the way Éarendil developed. Over time key themes became attached to the character, most notably that of love between men and elves, and the choices such love brings between the curses attendant on each race, death and deathlessness. You can also see Tolkien's concern to tie up the loose ends of English myth, to explain the many mysteries of Old and Middle English, and to create a single, unified 'ancient' culture that preserved the phenomena of what we have now, the fragments of a lost oral tradition. Earendil's name is of course one instance. The name that Tolkien bestowed on his ship was another. As early as 1917 and the first drafts of *The Book of Lost Tales* he had named it Wingelot, after Guingelot, the ship of a truly lost English figure, Wade, which itself echoes – or is echoed by – Gringelot, the name of Gawain's horse in *Sir Gawain and the Green Knight*, the 14th-century West Midlands poem that Tolkien later translated and edited.

It's quite clear that, even into the 14th century and beyond, Wade was part of the common store of early English culture. Geoffrey Chaucer refers to him twice, clearly assuming that his audience will know whom he was referring to. (An Elizabethan commentator on *The Canterbury Tales* decided not to elaborate on Wade as the tale was too 'long and fabulous'.) Wade is also a reference point for Sir Thomas Malory in the *Morte d'Arthur*. Yet because the stories were never written down, they have vanished. Wade seems to have surfaced from the sagas, where he was a man of great strength, possibly a giant, with an affinity for the sea, and, perhaps, someone who answered cries for help. Guingelot, too, appears to have had magical properties – the ability to ride over churches or sail under water. All these enrich the idea of Éarendil, connecting him to lost or forgotten traditions, rescuing them from oblivion.

Wade is at least remembered in our maps. There are several Wade-related sites in North Yorkshire, most notably the Wade stones, two menhirs that stand a mile or so apart about six miles outside Whitby. They were thought to mark the site of his grave. There is also Wade's Causeway across the Yorkshire Dales, which runs from Whitby south to Malton; that this is, in fact, a Roman road, tells you much about when Wade entered our folklore. Wade had a son, too, named Wayland, whom we shall meet again later.

Tolkien began to write prolifically after this holiday. Cornwall seems to have clarified for him where his interests and talents lay, but the war intervened.[3] Despite the squalor and filth of trench life, and despite, too, the fear – he was not, as he frequently confessed, a naturally courageous man, nor a good officer – he continued to develop his ideas. Not that his experiences in the trenches didn't provide ample subject matter too, as he recalled to the *Birmingham Post* in old age:

The war made me poignantly aware of the beauty of the world. I remember miles and miles of seething, tortured earth, perhaps best described in the chapter about the approaches to Mordor. It was a searing experience.[4]

It gave him, he said, a need to express what he felt about good and evil. That what came out was, if not escapism, then the translation of experience into symbol, the knowing creation of myth, is probably due to the particular moment in his life that was interrupted by war.[5] Contrary to what one might imagine, he had never had a particular liking for folk tales and fairy stories as a child. It was not until he came to them through his philological studies that his passion for them woke, and it would be stirred further by his experience of the horrors of war.[6]

What precisely was it in Cornwall that inspired him? What did he see down there? On one level trying to trace the influence of landscape on the creative mind of a young man in 1914, especially by following in his footsteps, is a curious and probably ridiculous thing to do. But the point isn't necessarily to try and envisage the landscape precisely as he might have seen it; rather, it is to view the world through the filter of his work, trying to understand what the relationship between the two might reveal of his imagination.

Walking was always a source of pleasure for Tolkien – one which he passed on to his children – and it is really the only way to experience the landscapes that he loved. Even when cars where commonplace he disdained them, although, given that when he was behind the wheel his approach to pedestrians was that of a cavalry officer riding down enemy infantry, that's probably no bad thing. Yet he was not what you'd call a hiker, despite the 20-odd miles he probably covered that one day on the Lizard. C.S. Lewis's brother Warren ('Warnie') said, as noted in Carpenter's *The Inklings*, that Tolkien's idea of a walk was no more than a stroll, prolonged by endless diversions into the botanical and other phenomena that nature provided. He sounds, in fact, like a rather more learned version of P.G. Wodehouse's Lord Emsworth pottering for ever in his beloved garden. Tolkien, for his part, thought the Lewis brothers' approach harsh and baulked at the heavy packs they insisted on carrying.

Despite the intervening 80 years Cornwall is still definitively, even defiantly, different from the rest of England. The coast, both north and south, is harsh and broken, the land exposed. All the elements are heightened. It feels like an island in itself, especially as the peninsula narrows and the strip of land between the two seas tails away. Yet in its sandy coves and sheltered bays, its green sheltered valleys, Cornwall has the warmth and intimacy of a refuge. It helps that, unlike other coastal holiday destinations in England, Cornwall is far from the reach of the big industrial cities. The mass tourism that transformed Blackpool or Bexhill or Margate has made no mark here. Popular though Cornwall is now, it is still on a small scale. Fishermen work the harbours where tourists browse the postcard stands and the motorway stops at Exeter.

The Lizard – also known as Kirrier, the high coast, one of the two Cornish hundreds (a hundred being a subdivision of an English shire dating from the eighth century) – is the southern-most point of mainland Britain. Due south is Spain's North Atlantic coast on the Bay of Biscay, roughly halfway between the French border and the pilgrims' destination of Santiago de Compostela or, for that matter, Phillip II's shipyards at Corunna. Due west is Newfoundland. Alboin, a central character in Tolkien's unfinished novel *The Lost Road,* rhapsodises about the experience of the sea – or, more accurately, of standing on the Cornish shore looking out to sea – wishing that it could stretch out forever without a coast to contain it on the other side. He regards it almost as a Platonic ideal, the perfect sea. It is no surprise that Alboin is quite clearly at least semi-autobiographical. If Tolkien's description of his character as beginning to learn Norse, Welsh, Irish and Old English when he was 15 were not evidence enough of Alboin's similarity to his creator, then there is also the fact that the history of languages in general, and of sound-changes in particular, are one of Alboin's hobbies.[7]

More than most of the coast down here, that which surrounds the Lizard is perilous. It boasts more shipwrecks than elsewhere along the southern coast. They were frequent events before the lighthouse was built. Down at the base of Lizard Point they were rebuilding the lifeboat-house for the third and final time when Tolkien walked here in 1914. It's not in use now, except as somewhere for local fisherman to stack their lobster pots, half-rusted, on the tracks, but evidence of the wrecks can still be found. Take the *Socoa*, bound for San Francisco with concrete to rebuild the city after the earthquake. It foundered in the sea off Cadgwith, a little northeast of Lizard Point, near the charmingly named Devil's Frying Pan, and its load still sits in the sea.

Proximity to that kind of danger lends darkness to the county's character. There is a wildness to Cornwall that survives the cream teas and the comfortable pubs. It was only in 1830 that Parliament allowed those who had died at sea to be buried in consecrated ground at the county's expense. Previously the dead and their unhallowed ghosts were a familiar presence. Daphne du Maurier, a resident of Falmouth, records a grizzly story in her *Vanishing Cornwall* concerning a transport ship that was wrecked off Lizard Point, several hundred corpses being washed ashore in the aftermath. The local people went down to the sea to find the drowned men, wrapped in seaweed or broken on the rocks, and bring them back one at a time up the narrow path from the beach for burial. As they dug the mass grave and continued their belated act of rescue they found themselves fighting off a pack of dogs drawn from miles around to scavenge among the dead. This may not be an especially charming anecdote, but it does at least dispel the romantic ideas one might have about rural England, particularly on its margins, worried as they are by all manner of discontents, historical and cultural, natural and supernatural.

I came to the Lizard towards the end of August, a little later in the year than Tolkien came. A heatwave that had laid low most of Europe was in its last days and the tourist season was tailing away in long traffic jams clogging the thin roads east, cars piled high with cases and beachwear, tired parents nursing along exhausted offspring, all reluctant to leave.

The Point itself, where England ends, has the perpetual drama of much of the Cornish coast, that vertiginous sense of the world falling away to nothing, the earth torn free of some speculative mooring. You can stand at the edge of the cliffs, the warm wind charging unsteadily around you, and see a sheer drop below your feet to the water below – seaweed-like vegetation, rusty, fire-coloured, cascading down the rock face. It's hard to be comforted by the iron pinnings that appear to hold it all together. Up at the top the fields are bordered with dry-stone walls laid, so a friend has told me, in 'herring-bone' style. Sheep graze up to the lip of the land, seemingly unconcerned. Round bales of hay litter the cropped fields and look like the toy building blocks of an outsize child; a little more wind, you feel, would send them rolling into the sea. Somehow the effect is marred by the craft shops selling clocks and barometers set in serpentine, the rock on which most of the peninsula rests. It's a local speciality and you are hard-pressed to find a shop in the village that isn't selling any. They've been working it commercially for around 170 years; I came across a reference in a *Parochial History of Cornwall* (1838) to 'a manufactory [that] has been recently established for producing ornamental trifles from the beautifully coloured and variegated serpentine'. It continues, ominously: 'They hope to polish chimney-pieces on a large scale.' Likewise, the guide ropes and railings that nurse you down the concrete path, wide enough, I noted, for two buggies to pass, leading down to the lifeboat house, practical though they are, do much to diminish the thrill.

But at the base of the cliffs – where the small fistful of sand is almost silver and the brightly coloured fishing boats, all boasting female names, are huddled together beneath the blank sky, drawn up into the shadow of the rocks to avoid the tide at its height – it is impossible not to look out, as Alboin does in Tolkien's unfinished novel, and feel the strangeness and possibilities of the sea, the palpable distance of its horizons, the lure of its power, its promise of escape. All the while the island is literally at your back, tall cliffs bearing down. You can press yourself against England and feel its ancient indifference dig into your flesh.

For most of us interest in English history begins with the written record, which the people of these islands enter into with the Roman empire and its colonial ambitions in the century or so before Christ. For Tolkien that record was merely the uppermost layer. In some respects his determined taste for antiquity is more in keeping with pre-modern thinking: there is almost a deference to age for its own sake. His interest was always directed to the point at which traditions of language and culture begin to be translated into documentary evidence, which also marks a moment of loss, things passing from memory uncaptured by the scribe.[8]

Humphrey Carpenter's biography records Tolkien's reaction to a walk down the length of the peninsula to the Point that he and Father Reade undertook one day. He was astonished by the protean quality of the landscape, noting that each valley seemed snatched from a different county. If you come south, as he did, you pass through Helford at the mouth of the eponymous river, an absurdly pretty and therefore now rather exclusive village rising out of the banks of the estuary, its southern half linked to the north by no more than a foot bridge, houses and gardens lapped by the waters. Fishermen can no longer afford to live here.

South of Helford the lush woodland that hides it gives way to pasture and then, abruptly, you are knee-deep in brush and scrub grass on the high plain at Goonhilly, an area of untended moorland skirted with small woods and coppices, civil congregations on the borders of the wild. Nowadays Goonhilly is synonymous with the satellite monitoring station. Even though such dishes are a commonplace sight, the station still has a compelling presence as an icon of technology amid the tumuli that scatter the moor. Indeed, just outside the station's wire fence is a standing stone, the Dry Tree menhir, some 10 feet tall (it used to be bigger but soldiers lopped three feet off the top during the First World War). When Tolkien came by it was still fallen, not being resurrected until later in the century. There ought by rights to be some kind of incongruity in such a juxtaposition, but actually it is rather beautiful, this companionship of human endeavour across the centuries. Now that the space race of the 1960s and 1970s is receding into memory there is an element of nostalgia too in the promise that we thought the Moon shots offered, collected here in the open faces of the satellite dishes, still scanning the skies in hope.

Looking back north from the stone you can see the green fields and hedges of what seems another England fading into the grey trees beyond. South of here the flatlands fall away steeply into the valley around Ruan Minor, and the narrow road you walk down – or drive down at your peril – is high-banked, hemming you in, robbing you of any horizon beyond a few feet. The road skims across cold, bright streams on broken-sided bridges and bores on through resisting woodland as the trees close over your head. Beyond, of course, is the coast. Tolkien went on to the Point that day, arriving at sunset to see the beam from the lighthouse arcing across the sky.

However, of all the places Tolkien visited that summer Kynance Cove, west of Goonhilly, is what impressed him most. He wrote about it at length to his fiancée and later in the year he wrote a poem about it, 'Sea Chant of an Elder Day', attempting to capture the power and mystery of the sea. (Carpenter quotes a little of it in his biography.) The poem is not especially good, and it remained not especially good when he lengthened it a couple of years later and incorporated it into his burgeoning mythology, recasting it as 'The Horns of Ulmo', in which Tuor, Earendil's father, tells his son about how he came to be the first man to set eyes on the sea.

Kynance is not somewhere you can go to be alone with your thoughts now, and certainly not in the summer. These days you come to it either on the Southwest Coastal Path or from the tidy car park at the end of a toll road. Either way you get down to the cove on a fresh gravel path laid over neatly placed rugged rocks, which is impossible to slip on except in the worst weather: a very National Trust, health-and-safety-conscious kind of path, built to counter the erosion caused by 20th-century tourism. True to form, it's crowded like a trunk road, with much polite English side-stepping and avoidance of eye contact.

At the top of the path the wind whistles fitfully in the tall, almost tropical grasses that rise from the rocks and the purple heathers. As you walk down the sound dies away and the arms of the bay open around you. Not that it's quiet. The air squalls with happy children, screaming with exhilaration in the cold Atlantic water; amateur surfers, half-hearted, lie hesitantly on their boards, barely riding the shallow waves.

I perch myself on an outcrop of rock above the bay to the south. It's hard to see the landscape clearly for the people, especially somewhere like here, where human activity seems incidental, irrelevant. The beach is of course busy, despite the less than perfect weather today. The sun is around from time to time, but the wind is brusque and chivvying, catching you unawares with its bite, as it often does in Cornwall. Being English, holidaymakers have come prepared, and the sand is spotted with wind-breakers and tents. An intrepid few have ventured into bikinis or trunks, but the mass are in t-shirts, jean shorts, jeans or khakis, mostly in fashionably soft military greens and beiges; the red fleeces and the synthetic blues and scarlets of the canvas, not to mention the swimsuits and towels, seem to come from another modern world.

Around me, if you ignore the discarded cans of Fosters lager, the rocks are like burnt timbers, blackened but touched here and there with traces of the pale colours you'd expect to find at the faded sea-side entertainments of the Sussex coast: burgundies bleached down to foundation-pink, blue-greens washed out to turquoise. Vivid green lichens slowly annex the cliff-face, thin streams skipping lightly between hunks of couch grass. A strange sense of ruin pervades the place: the hollowed cliffs guard the shallow waters like fallen gods, breathless now, exposed and unmoving. No one swims out beyond their reach.

The clouds are brisk, their shadows making the page I wrote on seem fluid. One or two seagulls dot the visible sea, a few more scrape the air, circling, turning to scavenge from the beach café's waste, their cries mixing with the shrieks of children in a proto-language of hunger and joy. The sea is featureless, a kind of blank canvas, emerald green out beyond the arms of the bay where the clouds move swiftly across the surface of the water, trails of light between them as if something hidden were rising to meet the air, like a line holding, not holding, against the darker, greyer waves that meet the eye combing the near-white horizon.

Actually, before the place where you expect sky and sea to meet there is a paler line, almost a shadow, a pale shadow that you want to mistake for a line of distant hills, another country. I'm reminded, as I always am looking out across the limitless sea, of the story of Sir John Ross, who in 1818 led an expedition in search of the Northwest Passage, the El Dorado of 19th-century naval exploration. To the barely suppressed disbelief of many of his officers, Ross winningly identified some low-lying clouds on the horizon as a range of mountains blocking the way through the western end of Lancaster Sound in Baffin Bay. His expedition thus apparently thwarted, he turned for home, naming his new mountain range after the First Lord of the Admiralty, John Wilson Croker. Sadly the courtesy did him little good when it was subsequently shown, by an expedition led by William Parry, one of his junior officers, that no such mountains existed and that there was indeed a passage through.

To the south and west of here, between Lizard Point and Mount's Bay over by Penzance, the remains of a submerged forest have been found, dating from the Bronze Age when the tide was further out than it is now. Interestingly, it is a fact that demonstrates the tenacity of folk memory, how accurate information can sometimes survive in folklore, however corrupted or apparently fanciful, over centuries. In Camden's *Britannia*, he says of Cornwall that:

The inhabitants do suppose that this promontory heretofore ran further into the sea [and] out of I wote not what fable, that the earth now covered over with the in-breaking of the sea was called 'Lyonesse'.

This is the sort of thing that Tolkien would have taken as vindication for his theory – or belief – that ancient languages, and in particular the areas in which they seemed difficult or problematic, offered clues to the unrecorded past. It is also a reminder of Tolkien's conception of Middle Earth, shaped around that theory, as existing at some indeterminate date in our prehistory when the land masses were shaped differently. It was important that this should not be impossible, that it should stay just this side of pure fantasy.[9] Although he later regretted not having pursued the idea with his usual zealous attention to detail, there is in any event a pleasing plausibility about it if you don't think about the evidence too hard, certainly for inhabitants of an island such as Britain, the borders of which, under siege as they are by the sea, have always been hard-fought, fluid, ephemeral. Over on the Suffolk coast Dunwich, once a thriving medieval harbour, has long since lost its battle and mostly now lies under the waves, while (as explored in Chapter 3) the Severn has spent the last two millennia in retreat from the quayside at Lydney.

Cornwall, I believe, presented a vital link for Tolkien in his development.[10] It seems to me more than a coincidence, for example, that the first known name for Cornwall is Belerion. I know Tolkien resisted strongly the idea that there were external influences on his languages and therefore his nomenclature, or that where they existed they were meaningful, but I am not sure that is necessarily true. The similarity to Beleriand is, I think, unarguable in any case. Cornwall was given that name by Diodurus Siculus, a Sicilian historian writing in Greek in the first century BC. That he also wrote about Atlantis makes me think it more likely than not that Tolkien came across him, given what he himself described as his Atlantis complex, part of which was a recurring dream of a tidal wave coming in high across fields and trees.

In any case, Cornwall provided an anchor for Tolkien's growing interest in the history of English, and its relationship with the various peoples and landscapes of these islands. It helped him to articulate for himself what his great project would be. In *The Lost Road* he writes of Alboin that he had always, ever since he had been a child, wanted to travel back in time to hear dead and forgotten languages spoken on the Atlantic coast, to meet the first men who walked there, to see the shape of the land, the lost kingdoms.[11]

Alboin imagines doing so in the Cornish holiday cottage he shares with his mysterious father, as if one day they could step outside the door and find themselves breathing prehistoric air.

The Lost Road, as far as it goes, is in fact steeped in Cornwall; it is hard to think of another county that offers the same intimate sense of antiquity. It seems peculiarly unscarred by history, a world to itself. There are, of course, castles and great houses here, and other signs of political power and dominion, but the continuities outweigh them. It was one of Tolkien's fondest literary beliefs that readers could sense the authenticity of names, especially place names, without really understanding why. It led him, for instance, to base the names around Bree on Welsh words, to distinguish it from the more English Shire. Archet is *ar chet*, the wood; Combe is from *cwm*, valley.[12] He could have taken Cornwall as an exemplar of his theory too: many names here are distinctive, different from anywhere else in England, because rooted more deeply in Brythonic Celtic (related to Welsh and Breton, but distinct from Goidelic Celtic, the group that comprises Irish, Scots Gaelic and the extinct language of the Isle of Man).

The other thing that, I suspect, Cornwall gave him was a sense of the sea. I wouldn't pretend for a minute that we can say that the Grey Havens may be confidently located anywhere in particular in the county. But I am sure we can say that it is somewhere very like a harbour in Cornwall. Tolkien's description of it is spare, to say the least. The most you can glean is that it is on a firth at the mouth of the River Lune. Now, there is a River Lune in Lancashire; we have touched on it briefly with regard to Nodens (in Chapter 3). It does indeed open out into a firth, or estuary. The connection seems simple, despite a nagging doubt that, whatever Tolkien's faults as a writer, obviousness when it comes to naming was not one of them. There was probably nothing he laboured over more.

Etymology is unlikely to help us. Lune is an old name. It pre-dates the Romans, for example. 'Lancaster', from the Roman name of the city, means no more than 'fort on the Lune'. 'Lune' itself means 'healthy' or 'bringer of health'. Yet the estuary itself feels otherwise. It is a bleak, wind-blasted place, overwhelmed with emptiness. Saltmarshes thick with scrub grass give way to mudflats where wading birds pick their way across the unstable land, pausing delicately to feed on the plentiful food burrowed too close to the surface. The whole opens out into Morecambe Bay. The estuary is perilous; there is quicksand to catch the unwary and the bay is in any case tidal. In spring the waters can rise by nine metres or more. Not much grows here and the few thorn trees that tenaciously grip the landscape are beaten things, bowed down by the unbroken force of the wind. The fields beyond are green and fertile; in the distance, on a clear day, you can see the hills of the Lake District grey on the horizon. Even in summer the wind is fierce, cold as steel. Winters must be bitter indeed.

Ultimately, I think, we have to take the view that the fact that Lancashire and Mithlond share a River Lune is a coincidence. I have no doubt that Tolkien was aware of it, but there seems to be no further significance to be drawn from the information. Tolkien's idea of the sea is different from what you encounter in Morecambe Bay. It is suffused with regret and longing, with departure and hope. All his early attempts at framing his myth for England involved a journey across the sea, whether by Aelfwine (essentially the same figure as Eriol, mentioned in the introduction) in *The Book of Lost Tales* or Alboin in *The Lost Road*, to Tol Eressëa, the Lonely Isle, or some version of it, where the mortal records the elven tales that eventually formed *The Silmarillion*. The elves had of course made the journey already, one from which they could not return. There are traces of Arthur's final journey to the Isle of Avalon in this, although on the whole Tolkien felt that, because the cycle of Arthurian myths is set in an already Christianised world, it is too impure to stand for England in the way that he wanted his own work to. There are echoes, too, of the Anglo-Saxon poem *The Seafarer*, quoted directly in *The Lost Road*, but a touchstone throughout for its sense of exile, mortality and loss. Aelfwine, in fact, is explicitly from Cornwall: in one draft he is an Anglo-Saxon driven out of England by the Normans. Later, in *The Notion Club Papers*, Tolkien has Lowdham and Jeremy set out from Land's End on their seaborne voyage into the past.

In *The Lord of the Rings* the most characteristic expression of Tolkien's love of the sea is the belief that, as Legolas explains to Gimli, the elves cannot rest easily in Middle Earth once they have laid eyes on the sea or even simply heard the cry of the gulls. It offers a kind of sadness, the prospect of loss, but it is also a means of redemption, carrying the path, the lost road, to Elvenhome, as well as being the means by which Earendil could go to plead for the peoples of Middle Earth. It's fitting that Tolkien's first draft of *The Lord of the Rings* ends with Sam returning home to Rose and hearing, as he closes the door, the soft, almost mournful sound of the sea lapping on the western shores.[13]

Chapter Five
Oxford, Sarehole, Moseley, Birmingham

In *J.R.R. Tolkien: A Biography* Humphrey Carpenter notes the irony that a man who spent his life writing about vast natural landscapes, with great sensitivity and greater love, actually lived exclusively in cities, usually in comfortable, if unremarkable, houses in suburban areas. One can understand this, from a practical perspective. Tolkien's livelihood was tied to two universities, Leeds for a few years in the 1920s and then Oxford for the rest of his life. But that doesn't stop it from still occasioning surprise.

One of the first things I did when I began work on this book was to visit Oxford, travelling the 60-odd miles from London by train from Paddington, then walking around the area in which Tolkien for the most part lived, a few blocks east of the Banbury Road. In particular I went to look at the two houses he lived in between 1925 and 1947, which are side by side at numbers 20 and 22 Northmoor Road. I didn't have any real expectation of startling insights, which was just as well. The visit certainly brought home the juxtaposition between Tolkien's extraordinary internal life, both intellectual and emotional, which found its outlet in his writing, and the extreme ordinariness of his day-to-day existence.

Number 22 is the smaller and more conventionally pretty of the two houses, and was the one which the Tolkien family lived in first. It is charming, with a green lawn sweeping round the red-brick walls, which are coated with lilac wisteria. Two immense and evidently overfed pigeons stood like sentinels on the wooden fence the whole time I was there, while a squirrel rummaged energetically in the undergrowth. When the family outgrew number 22, in 1930, they moved next door to number 20, a grey, wide and surprisingly featureless house spread imposingly along the east side of the road: imposingly, but also oddly unassertively. It stands out from most of the other houses in the road, which are typically solid, authoritative Victorian red-brick villas, their gardens brimming with bushes and shrubs. It was while the family was living at number 20 that Tolkien wrote most of *The Hobbit* and *The Lord of the Rings*. A small, discreet plaque marks the fact.

The River Cherwell is a few minutes walk away, through the gate of Lady Margaret Hall and into the University Parks. Tom Shippey argues that this river was Tolkien's inspiration for the Withywindle, on the basis both of a possible etymology of the name and of the Cherwell's character, particularly upstream of here, where it runs under overhanging willows – as the Withywindle does – on its way towards Wood Eaton.[1] It is an attractive idea and difficult not to accept on a damp fresh day in late spring, the overnight rain still bright on the stiff green grass, coots corralling their chicks in the dark, slow-running water. My only caveat would be that I had always felt the Withywindle represented a kind of archetypal English river, for the willows from which it derives its name ('withy' being an old synonym for 'willow') seem a quintessential part of any idyllic English summer landscape.

Walking back towards Northmoor Road, with the rumble of traffic on the Banbury Road ever-present, I couldn't help but reflect on how comfortable and unpoetic this small world was. To Tolkien's credit, however, he did try nevertheless to establish links between his everyday Oxford life and the world of his mythology in his unfinished time-travel novel of the 1940s, *The Notion Club Papers*, the contemporary sections of which are set in the city. I am not sure that it wouldn't have worked, if he had ever completed it, although coherently weaving the different eras together certainly presented an enormous technical challenge. Even in the sections that he completed the disjunction between, on the one hand, the quiet collegiate community and the neoclassical architecture of buildings such as the Radcliffe Camera, and, on the other, the arrival of the eagles of the Lords of the West in Numenor, is startling.

Ultimately, we shouldn't be too surprised that Tolkien lived in the kinds of places he did. More than most writers, he took his inspiration from literary or linguistic sources as much as from close observation of other people – or of nature for that matter. The way he synthesized the different elements, in particular the linguistic, was to a large degree an intellectual exercise; the creation and modification of languages could hardly be anything but. I have no doubt that he loved the English landscape and drew profound pleasure from his experience of it. However, it was not something he thirsted for in the way he did for language, which for him was the key to all his work. Where he lived was to a large degree irrelevant, a matter of functional necessity rather than a statement of character.

Yet Birmingham might be an exception to this pattern. Arguably England's second city now, it is certainly the major city of the Midlands. It is revealing, in fact, in how small an arc Tolkien lived most of his life. Birmingham is only 60 miles to the northwest of Oxford, but, apart from the war years and his five-year stint at Leeds, the two cities and their environs account for almost his entire life. The West Midlands were, in every way, home to him. Central to his sense of belonging were the childhood years he spent in Sarehole, to the south of Birmingham, which had a deep and abiding claim on his affection, and has an equally strong claim to be a key source of inspiration for his work.

In Tolkien's childhood, in the last years of the 19th century and the first years of the 20th, Sarehole was a small village outside the city, but it was long ago overtaken by the rolling wave of 20th-century urbanization. In fact, it has an excellent, even pre-eminent, claim to be the origin of the Shire. In this respect it has one inestimable advantage over all other claimants to the crown: Tolkien himself explicitly stated it as a fact on a number of occasions. He told journalist William Foster, for instance, that the Shire 'was inspired by a few cherished square miles of actual countryside at Sarehole, near Birmingham'.[2] Indeed, after 70 years he was still capable of lyricizing about its virtues with surprising intensity to the *Oxford Mail* in 1966:

> I could draw you a map of every inch of it… I loved it
> with an intensity of love that was a kind of nostalgia
> reversed. There was an old mill that really did grind corn
> with two millers who went straight into *Farmer Giles of
> Ham*, a great big pond with swans on it, a sand pit, a
> wonderful dell with flowers, a few old-fashioned houses
> and, further away, a stream with another mill… It was a
> kind of lost paradise.

Actually, the identification can be even more precise than that. Shippey goes to great lengths to illustrate the extent to which the Shire is a Victorian construct, citing as evidence the existence of a universal postal service there, something not introduced in Britain until 1840.[3] However, in reality you need look no further than Tolkien's letters for the truth of the matter, where he clearly states that the Shire is a Warwickshire village circa Queen Victoria's Diamond Jubilee, which takes us to 1897. The Diamond Jubilee marked the 60th year of Queen Victoria's reign and – implicitly or otherwise – the apogee of the British empire. Tolkien later recalled walking across the river-meadows of Sarehole towards Moseley Grammar School and seeing it illuminated in fairy lights as part of the celebrations, a thing of wonder to a young, already fatherless child.[4]

Yet how far do such truths take us? In this instance it simply raises a number of questions, most of which arise from the fact that Tolkien was only five years old in 1897. What he really means, therefore, is, surely, not that the Shire was based on the Sarehole of that year, but that it was based on adult recollections of a childhood at just that time, which is not at all the same thing.

This is particularly so when you consider the straightened and unusual – not to say sad – circumstances of Tolkien's childhood, and the paradisal shadow that it continued to cast across his life.

The young Tolkien moved to Sarehole with his recently widowed mother Mabel and his younger brother Hilary in the summer of 1896. If it seemed in later life to have been a kind of haven or oasis, then that is perhaps because, in a sense, that is what it was. When the family arrived all three were still in shock from the death of Arthur Tolkien, John Ronald's father, in February 1896. Although it might be easy to diminish the emotional impact of such a loss for him, aged only four and having not seen his father for a year, it is markedly harder to do so after reading the letter from son to father written the day before Arthur's faraway death, which is full of a young child's inexhaustible love for his parents.[5]

When the Tolkiens left Sarehole it was to move into a succession of small, sometimes dismal houses, while Mabel struggled to make ends meet on the modest sum left to her by her husband. She struggled further when her Baptist family ostracized her following her conversion to Catholicism in 1900. By the end of 1904 she was dead from diabetes, which was then untreatable. She died in the single room she shared with her sons, only 34 years old, exhausted by poverty and downcast because of her family's neglect of her, as Tolkien later bitterly recalled in a letter to his son Michael.[6] If Sarehole represented summer, light, warmth and childhood joy for him, everything from then on – already changed but now irrevocably so – became empty and cold.[7]

It is hard not to read the Cottage of Lost Play, the first framing device for his mythology in *The Book of Lost Tales*, as at the very least a reference to this period. Its central character is Eriol, a wanderer who comes to Valinor, the land of the Gnomes – here the diminutive figures of more traditional folklore – and finds the eponymous cottage, which, among things, children can come to in their sleep down the Path of Dreams. It's not entirely clear to me, but, as I understand it, the point is that the cottage restores to the children the play they have been deprived of. The personal applicability of this scenario is obvious; indeed, a related poem of the same title also, slightly strangely, seems to encompass Edith too. It is arguable that here we can sense the depth of the emotion that underlies Tolkien's wish for redress, while recognizing the unsuccessful, even embarrassing results. It is probably to everyone's advantage that Tolkien abandoned much of this device quite quickly, in particular turning against the idea of 'little folk' and restoring elves – or gnomes, as he persisted in calling them for some years yet – to more or less human dimensions.

Yet neither Sarehole nor the Shire, its literary shadow, truly offered paradise perfected by any means. For all his recollection of idyllic days in the still deserted countryside, Tolkien was rather less romantic about Sarehole than you might at first think. Given the synonymy with the Shire, this suggests a more complex and subtle creation than his critics usually allow him. Certainly, to some extent he regarded the Shire and its inhabitants as parodies, albeit affectionate parodies.[8] To the end of his life he also remembered quite clearly the unpopularity with which he and his brother were met, not least because of his mother's choice of clothes for them, as he told the *Oxford Mail* in 1966:

> I took the idea of the hobbits from the village people and
> children. They rather despised me because my mother
> liked me to be pretty. I went about with long hair and a
> Little Lord Fauntleroy costume.

Even at that early age Tolkien professed himself fascinated by the local people's dialect. One suspects that the fascination was not reciprocated.

That more troubled sense of place and identity, some of which catches the fine-tuned English ear for class distinctions, finds clear expression in the Shire, which, interestingly, seems to have a middle class and a rural working class, if not exactly a proletariat, but not much in the way of a nobility. Tolkien emphasizes well the native cynicism and suspicion of the English, especially when sandbagged by alcohol in that most conservative yet seditious English institution, the pub. I am thinking in particular of the scene in *The Lord of the Rings* that is set at the Green Dragon in Bywater, which, if nothing else, demonstrates that, for all that the Shire represents an ideal to Frodo and Sam, it actually falls some way short of Heaven in other regards.

Someone some day should write an article on Tolkien's favourite watering holes, supposing that his diaries reveal more than the sources currently in print do. The obvious place to start is the Eagle and Child in Oxford, famed, in some circles at least, as the preferred meeting place of the Inklings, the loose group of academics and writers that gravitated towards C.S. Lewis. While it is certainly a solid and comfortable place, with two snug bars for locals on either side of the front entrance and a parlour further back, in which the Inklings used to gather, it is hard to get too excited about it. Granted, I was there at lunchtime, so I may simply have failed to drink enough, but the thing that most endeared it to me was the astonishing lack of anything drawing attention to the fact that Tolkien and Lewis drank there. It's not that there was nothing, simply that what there was comprised little more than some old black-and-white portrait photos, together with a handful of framed and yellowing paper clippings on the wall above their favourite corner. You have to get right up close to read the information – no indiscreet signage here – which is likely to be to the irritation of anyone sitting beneath, if my experience is anything to go by. Only in England, I thought, could somewhere that presumably caters at least a little to the tourist trade make so little effort to capitalize on a link with not one but two of the world's most popular authors.

The opposite is true of the Shireburn Arms in Hurst Green in the Ribble Valley (see Chapter 6). I think it is fairly well-established that Tolkien drank there, not least because there wasn't a great deal of choice if he found himself with a thirst when staying at Stonyhurst. But it is hardly central to his intellectual life, which the Eagle and Child – or the 'Bird and Baby', as they fondly called it – undoubtedly was, through the auspices of the Inklings. However, I suspect that his favourite pub was not the Eagle and Child. It didn't have a monopoly on his trade when he was in Oxford, after all. The King's Arms, the Mitre and the White Horse were also frequented. On the other hand, he went out of his way in an interview in 1967 [9] to talk about the Trip to Jerusalem in Nottingham. As he notes, it is England's oldest pub, dating back to the 12th century. Even more extraordinary is the fact that it is carved out of the solid rock beneath Nottingham Castle. 'I went to Nottingham once for a conference,' he confided to the journalist. 'I fear we went to the Trip to Jerusalem and let the conference get on with itself.'

Such digression aside, a sense of loss seems to have always been central to Tolkien's emotional life. It is particularly evident in his writing about the English landscape and about the landscape of his childhood – and it seems to have been a constant from a very early age. He was hypersensitive to the prospect of destruction, especially when it seemed to be pursued with wanton mindlessness:

> There was a willow hanging over the mill pool and I learned to climb it. It belonged to a butcher on the Stratford Road, I think. One day they cut it down. They didn't do anything with it; the log just lay there. I never forgot that.[10]

He was heart-broken to revisit Sarehole in 1933 and find it, in his estimation, drowned in a sea of red brick, the scarce scenery of a happy childhood brutally stamped out by the blight of urban expansion.[11]

It is slightly surprising, then, to visit the area now. While it has unarguably been surrounded by the city, it certainly has not been engulfed by it. Quite the opposite: it seems a kind of island of its own, resistant somehow to the tide. True, the approach still has the capacity to depress, even for someone like me who has lived in a city his whole life. It is not that the southern suburbs of Birmingham are uniquely grey; they are simply typically so.

Although the store fronts may change, you could be in any one of a number of cities or towns across the country. The big-brand retail heavyweights may not have ventured here, but that hasn't made for much in the way of distinctiveness among those stores that have.

I came from the southeast along the Stratford Road, through suburban Shirley on the outskirts of the city. It was a clear, wet early summer day, the rain still crisp and cold in the air even though the sun was shining. I turned left down Cole Bank Road and crossed a roundabout. Suddenly there on the right was the mill, Tolkien's precious mill, half-hidden from the road but still substantially as it used to look 100 years ago. I am tempted to say that if you half-close your eyes you can almost see two small boys laughing, dodging the cart carrying bags of flour to market, running from the dusty roar and the clenched fist of the miller or his son. The truth is that the traffic moves too fast along the road to indulge such notions and at the moment of that first glimpse of the mill the peculiar, spectral immediacy of imagination has gone.

Quite why the town planners left Sarehole Mill untouched, to complicate the tidy clarity of their plans, I don't know. Perhaps the ground between the mill-pond and the River Cole is simply too wet to build on. This is certainly the only place I know where a river is forded by a suburban road. Just to the north of the open ground in the right angle between Wake Green Road and Sarehole Mill, Green Road meets the River Cole. Usually the water would simply be fed through a tunnel beneath the road, but not here: the slope is too steep. Even in high summer, when, I imagine, the river is pretty much at its lowest ebb, vehicles still have to be cautious.

The water was more than a foot deep when I was there, standing in the shade of the trees watching the car's nervous progress and wondering if the river ever threatened to flood the adjacent houses. A marker seemed to indicate that the water can rise to an alarming height.

The area that had the greatest significance to Tolkien in his childhood was the swatch of land that runs north from the mill up to Moseley Bog. It is understandable that he should be shocked at the extent of the building that had taken place by the time he revisited Sarehole in 1933. It had raced up in the years after the First World War. But, temperament aside, if he had revisited more frequently he might have been pleased at how much survived. As with all the great cities of England, vast tracts of what we now call 'green belt' were swallowed up in the 1920s and 1930s, capitalizing on the growth of tram or suburban train links, and catering to younger generations of men and women who saw their identities as increasingly urban – whether through choice or necessity – and who, unlike Tolkien, were inclined to see the acres of new homes and fresh tarmac roads as symbols of progress, prosperity and happiness. The red-brick houses whose existence Tolkien bemoaned were not slum tenements, after all, but decent-sized family homes – significantly better, I imagine, than some of the places he lived in in Birmingham after he was parted from Sarehole.

There is a satisfying neatness – or, if you prefer, a kind of poetic closure – to the fact that, when an appeal was launched in 1960 to save the mill, Tolkien was able to offer his support, thanks to the financial success of *The Lord of the Rings*. The miller's house had in fact been occupied until the previous year, although the property as a whole was by then owned by Birmingham City Council, owing to a bequest in 1946. The mill had been active until as late as 1919, when the urbanization of what is now a southern suburb of Birmingham was well under way, but Tolkien's recollections of it as a corn mill reflect only a small part of its history.

The first mill on the site was built in 1542, the year that saw the births of Francis Drake and Mary, Queen of Scots. Henry VIII was on the throne of England, declaring war on Scotland and having his fifth wife, Catherine Howard, beheaded. Birmingham was already a prosperous town, with perhaps 1,500 inhabitants. Although it had established itself as a regional centre for the wool and leather trades, metalworking was already a major part of its culture, buoyed by strong sources of iron ore and coal, and the good number of rivers and streams for mills to power the forges. William Camden, writing a few decades later in his *Britannia* – one of the first serious attempts to assimilate the history and geography of England – described Birmingham as 'full of inhabitants, and resounding with hammer and anvils, for most of them are smiths. The lower part thereof standeth very waterish.' Indeed, although Sarehole Mill started out, as it ended, as a cornmill, during its working life of not quite 400 years it was also used for producing sheet metal, grinding blades, wire-drawing and grinding bones for fertilizer, reflecting the twin local economies, rural and urban.

The mill as it stands now does not date from that period, however, but from the late 18th century, when it was entirely rebuilt. The restoration, while clearly a huge success, nevertheless has the effect of making the mill seem smarter and more prosperous than perhaps it really was. Certainly in Tolkien's day, after 100-odd years of work, the building must have been considerably less neat and trim; at least one former owner went bankrupt. Now it looks as much a museum as a mill, if not more so. Like many industrial heritage projects, it preserves the form of things while draining them of the meaning that came from their use.

It was the industrial revolution that really saw Birmingham explode and that gave it the pre-eminence it still enjoys today over the other cities of the Midlands, such as Warwick, Derby or Leicester. It was expanding rapidly in the late 19th century as much as it was to do in the early 20th. The late 1870s, for instance, saw the construction of the Bournville estate at what was Bournbrook, just a few miles to the west of Sarehole, a massive undertaking that included the eponymous chocolate factory, as well as houses, schools and other facilities for the thousands of Cadbury's workers. Perhaps it all seemed remote to a young, poor boy like Tolkien, distant like the hard, dark city itself four miles to the north. It may be fanciful, but I did wonder if there was nevertheless an echo of Bournville in an early draft of *The Lord of the Rings* dating from 1939, or more accurately a preliminary sketch for a draft. Looking into what later became the mirror of Galadriel, the hobbits see a biscuit factory built in place of the old mill in their beloved Shire.[12] Of course, this scene failed to make it into the final version, though whether because it appeared unduly bathetic and insufficiently sinister, or too specific, or simply wrong, it is impossible to know. If Tolkien did know Bournville, he must have felt that it belonged to another world.

You can still sense the limits of Tolkien's childhood world today, circumscribed as it is in a square mile or two. The house he lived in in Sarehole still stands, roughly equidistant between the mill and Moseley Bog, where a gentle hill begins to rise towards the city. Its address now is 264 Wake Green Road, although in Tolkien's day it was 5 Gracewell. Apart from the small group of houses to which it belongs, everything else you see when you stand outside it has been built in the century or so since Tolkien left, the fields beneath long obliterated, the vistas interrupted or broken. The house itself is often described as a small cottage, not least by Tolkien himself, but it is not what most people would recognize as such. It's a fairly sizeable, high-gabled, semi-detached house, built of red brick on the ground floor, white plaster on the first floor, and set back from what, even then, before the serious arrival of the motor car, must have been a major route for Birmingham and Stratford traffic. The road hasn't been appreciably widened since it was mapped by the Ordnance Survey in 1904.

Tolkien also described the house as old-fashioned, which again seems a pleasingly retrospective judgement. In 1897 it was only a couple of decades old. To my mind, it doesn't pretend to be anything other than late Victorian, almost Edwardian in style, owing a little, perhaps, to the then-voguish Arts and Crafts movement. It is now privately owned; if there is any kind of memorial plaque I didn't spot it.

To reach the mill from the house you cross the road and cut through an uninspiring field that would seem to be some kind of municipal recreation ground if it were not for the absence of any facilities, unless you count benches. Then you step across a small bridge over the tailrace of the mill and head for the museum. It is an imposing three-storey building, although, as the guidebook says, it makes more sense to think of it as simply the housing for a primitive machine. Corn was winched up to the attic floor, or garner; fed down to the stone floor below, where it was ground; and then collected on the bagging floor where the miller logged its weight before despatching it.

We are quite attuned now to thinking of industries powered by what is essentially a renewable energy source as necessarily beneficent: gentle, quiet pursuits from a more natural and harmonious time. It must have seemed different – more ambiguous – to a young child in the last years of Victorian England, never mind the millers who worked here then, a father and son who appear to have taken a dislike to the Tolkien boys, and whose appearance, heavy with flour dust, led the boys to label the younger one the white ogre.[13] The great millstones and, more so, the gears are brutal things, and even now the sense of being inside the mechanism of some primitive engine is strong. Everything seems disproportionate, outsized: gearwheels, which I associate with the delicate, miniature universe of a wristwatch, here are massy, all weight. They seem a clumsy, almost absurd response to the problem of refining grain to powder. One of the two waterwheels here – the North, which is some 200 years old – is 12 feet tall.

The museum is too quiet. There were perhaps a dozen visitors there the day I went, all of us treading softly on the wooden floors and gingerly climbing the steps. As in most museums you feel a little as if noise would be disrespectful. After all, everyone has come essentially to venerate the past, or its objects, to feed a vague, undefined, uneasy sense of awe at lost patterns of living. Yet the mill must have been a grim place to work in, with the stones grinding against one another, the gears squawking, moaning as the water pushed energy and tension through the machine.

Chased out of the mill by the white ogre or his black-bearded father, Tolkien would take refuge on the other side of the pond, where the mill's headrace comes in from the south, watching swans glide across the dark untroubled surface, climbing the trees, forgetting the low roar of the grinding floor over the water. Even now, when you look out across the pond from the mill the calm seems unreal. There were no swans when I visited and no wind to stir the leaves; a heron stood watch on an islet towards the further bank and kingfishers dived in the shadows.

The mill is a remarkable survival, really, as layers of history have piled up around it. But no less remarkable is Moseley Bog, a mile or less to the north, back past 5 Gracewell. I don't necessarily sub-scribe to the opinion that this is the basis for the Old Forest, Tom Bombadil's domain on the borders of the Shire. It's quite possible, of course, but direct evidence is thin on the ground. Yet it did offer Tolkien his first protracted encounter with English woodland, a love of which permeates all his work, and for that reason alone it is worth exploration.

I had come back later in the summer to visit Moseley Bog and had more or less assumed that you could walk to it from the mill. There's nothing on any map to indicate that you can't. However, I walked up and down Wake Green Road a few times, in a fruit-less search for a gate in the fence, before finally asking someone tending his garden for directions. He seemed used to being asked the question. Maybe it is simply the nature of the bog, but I found it hard to orientate myself through even once I'd located it. I'd parked my car in a small area on the peak of the hill behind the bog. A yellow-brown field of trim, rain-starved grass led down to the woods, bordered with rough, thick clumps of rye. It was just after noon. The air was sensual, enfolding, warm, heavy with pollen and slow with the summer heat. The sky was mostly veiled with thin cloud. As I walked down the hill towards the trees I noticed some scattered poplars rising high above the hazy green of the surrounding woods. A young Asian couple sat embracing on a discreet bench in the shade of the first trees, he in denim, she in the black headscarf of Islam. They started nervously as I stepped through the clearing, wondering exactly where I was going.

The next clearing I came to had a signpost, neatly shaped like a spearhead, with arrows guiding you straight ahead. Unfortunately, the point it indicates is precisely where the path forks to left or right. Perhaps it doesn't matter which you choose. I went for the right. It takes you through arches of hawthorn, where the trees have curled themselves like cats around the path, providing green light and green shade as you inspect the thick woods to your left. The foliage is dense and the shadow is commensurately deep. The tree trunks are shrouded in creepers and vines, and orange-red berries rise like a dubious gift from the ground.

It is no sylvan Arcadia. No sunlight cascades through the trees onto a forest floor carpeted with soft, springy moss. Moseley Bog is dark, old and enclosed – a small remaining part of the ancient English forests that stretched across much of the island. As late as 1980 archaeologists discovered here the site of a burnt mound that they dated to the middle of the Bronze Age, somewhere between 1500 and 1000 BC; and in the stream heat-shattered stones have been found that can be carbon-dated more precisely, to 1100 BC. Almost nothing is known about the peoples whose culture this mound belonged to; it predates even the first Goidelic wave of Celtic invasions, around the turn of the first millennium BC. But we know at least that mounds like this had many functions, providing heat for cooking, boiling water, cloth production, leather-working and, for that matter, saunas. (Indeed, this must make an excellent place for saunas.) You can taste the age of the place in the air: it is dark and wet and musty, stale like a long-locked room. I happened to be here on one of the hottest days of a hot summer and it may feel remarkably different at other times of the year. I don't think I imagined the claustrophobia, however: down at the heart of the bog, where the streams knot over the wet earth, everything is damp, sweaty and close. The fact that the rest of the country – of the continent, even – was parched, almost petrified in the record temperatures, while Moseley remained sodden underfoot, speaks volumes.

It is easy to imagine the excitement of the Tolkien brothers when they explored here. It feels remote, a private kingdom, even now. After my eyes had adjusted to the gloom I had no difficulty mistaking for something else more alluring the glint of sunlight breaking through the trees to spark on the curling water of the stream. It is a still place; sudden movement, any movement, catches the eye. If there is anything to stop you identifying more completely with the young Ronald it is probably the way the site has been modified to accommodate the growing number of tourists. Sections of the path are on raised boards, covered with something like chicken wire, presumably to prevent slipping. In places the banks of the stream are shorn up by slender branches woven together into a fence of kinds, which reminded me of nothing more than the basket-weaving we did at primary school. The sweet sodden smell of the wet reeds instantly flooded back, along with other memories.

Mostly what I took away was the sense of the weight in the air, its heady, not entirely healthy pressure. That brought me back, albeit reluctantly, to the Old Forest. Usually in Tolkien's writings, nature, when uncorrupted by the Saurons or Sarumans of the world, is beneficent, morally good. Where the trees are feared, as many fear those in Fangorn, it is because of ignorance and superstition. In the Old Forest, however, in Bombadil's domain, there are real malevolence and a dark brooding heart. If you want to, you can project the sensibilities of Tolkien's work onto the landscape. It is less easy to discern the threads leading in the opposite direction. But if anything unites the reality with Tolkien's fiction it is the sense of age that permeates both Moseley Bog and the Old Forest, encompassing things unchanging – a rarity in the largely manufactured English landscape – and the drowsy, enervated decay that arises from such stasis, which might simply be vegetal, but which Tolkien enlarges to a moral condition too.

There are other areas around Birmingham with strong Tolkien connections. These include a number of the houses he lived in after his mother died, mostly in Edgbaston. Although he was not quite poor, and attended the grammar school on a scholarship, there's little doubt that he and his brother lived close to poverty.

Then, outside Birmingham, there are the Lickey Hills. Tolkien certainly knew the hills well: he sometimes visited them with Edith when they were courting in secret. Indeed, on the fateful day when Father Francis finally uncovered their relationship, they had been out riding their bikes in the hills before repairing to Rednal for tea.[14]

Rednal must have had bittersweet associations for Tolkien. He had first arrived there with his mother and brother in June 1904, partly at least so that Mabel could convalesce. The three shared a room in a postman's cottage near the grounds of the Catholic Oratory. For a while it was almost idyllic, despite Mabel's ill health. But it was only a few months later, in November, that Mabel died. She is buried in the Catholic cemetery in Bromsgrove, to the south of the Lickey Hills. It is a simple grave under a stone in the shape of a Celtic cross.

It is not surprising, given all of the above, that Birmingham is working increasingly hard to promote its associations with Tolkien. Aside from an informative website, for instance, it has begun to hold annual Tolkien days at the mill. It is a shame, however, with all that it does have to offer, that the city is continuing to laud what it describes as 'the Two Towers'. There are certainly two of them, rising above the cramped houses of Edgbaston where Tolkien spent his adolescence. But there, really, the similarity ends. The towers in question are Perrot's Folly and the Waterworks. The first dates from 1758 and is some 96 feet tall. The story is that it was built by a wealthy businessman, John Perrot, so that he could see the grave of his wife 10 miles away. Unfortunately, the calculations were flawed, failing to allow for the varied height of the land in between: hence the fact that it is called a folly. The second, as you might expect, belongs to Edgbaston Waterworks and dates from the latter part of the 19th century. Both are red-brick. The latter is square; the former is itself made up of two towers, a narrow, round one adjoining a wider hexagonal one, which is square at its base.

I know there is some debate as to which actually are the two towers referred to in the title of the second volume of *The Lord of the Rings*, given that there are at least four candidates: Isengard, Minas Tirith, Cirith Ungol and Minas Morgul. That is one reason why Tolkien fought against using the title *The Two Towers*: it presented a needless ambiguity. However, he himself thought that it should be taken to refer to Saruman's tower of Orthanc at Isengard and to Cirith Ungol. The descriptions of these towers are, of course, easily accessible, as are Tolkien's drawings of the former, since they have been reprinted in *Sauron Defeated*. But if there is any relationship between them and what can be seen in Birmingham's two towers, it is certainly not striking.

Chapter Six
The Ribble Valley, Lancashire

I think it's reasonable to hold the position that the counties of the West Midlands represented a kind of spiritual home to Tolkien. However, that shouldn't be taken to mean that the region had anything like an exclusive claim on his affections.

Take the Ribble Valley up in Lancashire, for instance, 100 or more miles north of Birmingham and perhaps 30 miles north of Manchester. There is no doubt that Tolkien went there, and did so frequently, during the period when he was writing *The Lord of the Rings*. Specifically, he visited Stonyhurst College, for his eldest son, John, was then studying for the priesthood in the adjoining St Mary's Hall (now a prep school). Stonyhurst itself is one of the premier Catholic schools in England, with a heritage dating back more than 400 years, albeit not on these premises, which it acquired as recently as 1794. Unlike the better-known Ampleforth, it is not attached to a religious order. It is the biggest independent school under one roof, housing an extraordinary 525 rooms, which should give you some idea of the size of the place. Sir Arthur Conan Doyle is one of its more famous alumni, although three other former pupils are now saints, which may put the creation of Sherlock Holmes in an interesting perspective. I suspect that Tolkien would have been amused that the five academic years at Stonyhurst are called, respectively, Lower Grammar, Grammar, Syntax, Poetry and Rhetoric.

Lancashire as a whole has longstanding associations with conservatism in general and the 'old faith' in particular. It was notable for recusancy during the reign of Elizabeth I and is studded with the 'safe' houses used by Catholic priests sent from the English Seminary at Douai to try to raise the country against the Queen and her heretical religious settlement. Shakespeare may have spent his 'lost years' teaching at one such house, not many miles from Stonyhurst, at Hoghton. In the middle of the following century Stonyhurst itself was requisitioned by Oliver Cromwell the night before his victory at the Battle of Preston. It is said that he slept in full armour on a wooden table that had been dragged into the middle of a vast, marble-floored first-floor room so that, if anyone came in to attempt to assassinate him, he would be woken by their footsteps. The house was smaller then, with an oddly asymmetrical, foreshortened design: Cromwell described it as the finest half-house in England.

During the Second World War the English Seminary, the institution that prepares men for the priesthood, was evacuated from Rome to Stonyhurst for the duration of hostilities. Tolkien himself regularly came to stay for three or four weeks at a time, living in what is now the deputy master's house but was then the visitor's lodge. He signed the visitor's book several times between 1939 and 1941. Naturally, having an Oxford professor staying did not escape the school's attention and he was occasionally dragooned into giving the odd lecture, but for the most part he spent his time writing and indulging his love of the English countryside on long walks around the valley. The classroom in which he taught is now a computer room. The small room he was given to write in, meanwhile, is a 'technical room', which seems to mean here, as it often does elsewhere, that it is a space for the IT department to fill from floor to ceiling with old or broken computers and boxes of toner cartridges. I couldn't get in to see the room, but I suspect that I wouldn't have been able to see much anyway. When I looked up at it from outside it seemed rather abandoned.

Aside from the obviously propitious timing, there are other suggestions that Tolkien was inspired by Stonyhurst and its environs. The strongest of these is the college's visitors' lodge, which appears, bean plants and all, in *The Fellowship of the Ring* as Tom Bombadil's cottage in the Old Forest. We can say this with some certainty because Tolkien drew it himself (it appears in *The Pictures of J.R.R. Tolkien*) and labelled it as such. But the directness of this source may be beguiling in its clarity, giving a warning against too great a simplification, against the temptation to infer wider meaning from the fact of the connection. Bombadil himself originated in a toy doll that Tolkien's children acquired at some point in the early 1930s and had made his first appearance – along with Goldberry, Willowman and the barrow wights – in 'The Adventures of Tom Bombadil', a poem that Tolkien wrote before even *The Hobbit* had been published. But he was also intimately and explicitly associated in Tolkien's mind with somewhere else entirely. Bombadil, he wrote to his publisher in 1937, is a *genius loci* for the countryside of Oxfordshire and Berkshire, which Tolkien felt to be disappearing almost as he wrote.[1]

We deal elsewhere with his love affair with those two counties (see Chapters 8 and 9), but the character of Tom Bombadil merits further investigation, not only because of his possible links to Stonyhurst but also because of his anomalous position in *The Lord of the Rings*. From early on Tolkien corresponded with readers who were unsettled, or just plain irritated, by Bombadil. Indeed, the consensus seems to be that his entry into the narrative and the hobbits' challenges in the Old Forest are little more than tedious diversions en route to where the story really begins, at Rivendell. Bombadil, the thinking goes, was more or less shoehorned into the book because Tolkien felt that the hobbits ought to have some kind of adventure at that point and had this ready-made character that he could use. On this reading, Bombadil is a galumphing caricature of a nature spirit who doesn't even have the merit of fitting neatly into the schemata of Middle Earth. To this day Tolkien websites carry heated threads and learned essays on the subject of who he actually is and whether he deserves his place in the book anyway.

For me, however, Bombadil was always an attractive figure, even though – or perhaps because – he verges on the ridiculous. He brings a disruptive, uncertain, almost carnivalesque element to the narrative. There was, therefore, undoubtedly a strange thrill about standing outside 'his' cottage on a late, misty midsummer morning, at the end of a track perhaps half a mile from the main school building, past a thin copse and up the slight incline to a gate onto an empty lane. It is just as Tolkien drew it: a solid, square yellow-grey stone house, dating from around 1913, and set between the muddy track and some clotted brambly woodland. Surrounding it is a smallish and – from what I could see – fairly functional garden. It is, in fact, much that Bombadil's house isn't. In particular, it is prosaic. It is a fine and comfortable place to live, I am sure, but some way from the haven of hospitality and grace, the place of safety and exemplary husbandry, that Tolkien presents to us. This contrast in itself points to one of the problems in reading Tolkien's writings back into his source landscapes. There is of course a fascination in seeing how he fashioned and refashioned places to serve what he would have called his 'sub-creative' purposes ('*sub*-creative' because, for him, creation was reserved for God alone). The disjointed sense of seeing two things at once – the real and the projected – can bring the country and the things it holds to a strange and vivid kind of life. But there is always the danger of disappointment, that sense of anticipated pleasure being punctured in an instant.

The object of a journey like mine was to identify places that can add meaning to what is already inherent in Tolkien's work. The risk I took was that at the end of the journey there would be merely the thing itself, a natural feature or man-made object set in a landscape, which would have no real significance because in his use of it Tolkien transformed it utterly, so it would be ultimately arbitrary and perversely meaningless.

Seeing the ordinary and, to me, distinctly uninspiring model for Tom Bombadil's house made me think again about Bombadil himself. He is, after all, a myth within a myth. Even in the world of the book he is an enigma: his domain is otherworldly and mysterious; his will is quixotic. He operates outside the narrative rules that Tolkien had laid down, being unaffected by the Ring's gravitational pull and immune to the powers it bestows. By rights, then, Tolkien should have edited him out. Bombadil distorts the story both by his presence in the narrative and, more generally, by his presence in Tolkien's sub-created world.

That, however, seems to be Tolkien's point. Bombadil's timelessness and the irrelevance of the ring quest to his world disturbs the balance of the book and disrupts the obviously Manichean order, pushing something strange and eternal up through the carefully constructed superstructure of the story. It is one of the measures of Tolkien's artistic success that Middle Earth can contain and sustain such contradictions. There is no logic to Bombadil's presence and he is none too convincingly explained away at the Council of Elrond. It is as if they don't quite understand what he is doing in the story either. Yet there he still is. Tolkien acknowledged the peculiarity of his character, but felt that the book would simply be the poorer for his excision (*Letters*, p192).

One thing Bombadil certainly brings is a genuine sense of mystery, something he has in spades. In a world that is presented in minute detail, quasi-academic textual paraphernalia and all, and that exists at a fixed point in our prehistory, Bombadil reaches back to the very beginning, before the first foot stepped on Middle Earth. Perhaps there is a reason why his land borders the Shire: it is what exists on the other side of safety, with terrors, and their defeats, being dependent on an arbitrary, forgetful god, his indifference a mirror to the forest's malevolence, both of them rooted in time immemorial, beyond record. Our notional relationship to

the Third Age of *The Lord of the Rings* is much like its peoples'
relationship to Bombadil. Among other things, I guess, this brings
us closer to the actors: we share, at last, a perspective.

What did this have to do with the Ribble Valley? I intended to
find out. After all, the local council has enthusiastically created a
Tolkien trail for people to follow, some of which certainly suggests
a correspondence with the Shire. There has been a good deal of
media coverage of this trail, due in no small measure to the ener-
getic proselytizing of Jonathan Hewat, who is, among other
things, the marketing and admissions manager at Stonyhurst. He
makes an excellent case for the area's influence on Tolkien's work,
and has been sought out by innumerable newspapers and magazines. His office was my first port of call.

Jonathan is a tall, dark-haired Scot, who talks with charm and
confidence about both Tolkien and the Ribble Valley in a soft
Edinburgh accent. He used to teach and speaks with a measured
authority. Aside from kindly taking the time to show me around
the school, he also talked me through the history of Tolkien's connection to the area and some of its possible influences on the creation of the Shire. It was Jonathan who pointed out the identity
of Bombadil's house to me. He argues, persuasively, that the similarities between the map of the Shire and the way its rivers
Brandywine, Withywindle and Shirebourn converge, and that of
the Ribble Valley, with the Hodder, the Ribble and the Calder, are
too close to be just coincidence. Of course, once you accept that
link, you start to look for other similarities. Is Mitton Wood to the
east really the Old Forest, for instance? Hence the trail.

I wanted to believe him. It wasn't just that the valley itself feels sequestered, not quite a backwater but still a secluded, private place, slightly passed by. It was also the vague hope that there might be some greater meaning lurking behind the various meeting points between reality and fiction. That is not to say that I'd buy into some of the media coverage of the valley, which has tended to imply a rivalry with Sarehole, as if there could be only one single unambiguous answer to the complex question of influence.

It would be dull indeed if Tolkien's anointing of his childhood home as a central source automatically excluded the possibility of borrowings from elsewhere. Take, for instance (although it is outside the remit of this book), the creation of the Misty Mountains for *The Hobbit*, and Bilbo's adventures in them. These were largely based on a holiday Tolkien had with some friends in Switzerland in 1911, walking through the Bernese Alps before he went up to Oxford. Tolkien mentions in a letter that they started out from Interlaken and made their way to Zermatt by way of Meiringen and Brig. Celebdil, in the Misty Mountains, is based on the Silberhorn.[2]

However, it may be that, as some have suggested, Pendle Hill, at the southeastern end of the Ribble Valley, is another source for the Misty Mountains. This is a thought that has occurred to Jonathan. As we walked back from Tom Bombadil's house towards where I'd parked my car, the hill, which, at 2,000 feet, is the highest point in Lancashire, was wholly obscured by mist. Its dark, overbearing reputation precedes it, however. Jonathan turned to me, waving a hand in its direction. At least, that's where he said it was. I just couldn't tell. 'You never know, perhaps that's the inspiration for

the Misty Mountains,' he said. He may be right. The definitive-
ness of one source does not preclude the possibility of another
source, despite the absence of any direct link between Tolkien and
this area until after the writing and publication of *The Hobbit.*

It was lunchtime when I left Stonyhurst. I wasted no time in
taking up Jonathan's suggestion that my first port of call should be
the Shireburn Arms in the nearby village of Hurst Green. There
was the name, for one thing. Once you have named somewhere
the Shire, of course, putting a River Shirebourn within it is hardly
a great imaginative leap: 'bourn(e)' is a common enough English
river name, derived from a Celtic word for 'stream' that also gave
rise to the Scots word 'burn'. It could, then, be just a coincidence.
Or it could simply have been a little in-joke for Tolkien and his
son, and, perhaps, a few other intimates. Or it could be a clue, a
key to a small secret about the Shire. The problem with this way
of thinking – that there are secret concordances that can be
unlocked by those with the right key – is that it's the code-
breaker's approach to literature, the same well-spring that nour-
ishes the 'Shakespeare wasn't Shakespeare' conspiracy theorists.
This approach is more or less entirely at odds with what is known
of Tolkien's intentions, and, for that matter, with his character and
tastes.

In any event, as I sat in the garden looking down over the green
sheep-strewn fields to the cloudy beyond, I wondered: was this the
Shire? In some ways it reminded me more of the lush green of the
New Zealand locations used in Peter Jackson's cinematic version of
The Lord of the Rings than of the more measured, husbanded
beauty that Tolkien describes in his work. Despite the fine, dark

beer there was only one way to find out for sure. I crossed the road and began the trail.

Instantly I was lost, having set off confidently in the wrong direction from the pub. The leaflet I had said that I should start with my back to it, and so I did. It didn't specify where, however. I realized pretty much straightaway that I had made a bad decision – some locals were standing and staring for one thing, and for another I hit a 'no entry' sign. I stubbornly pressed on anyway, with a short cut of my own, thinking that it would all come clear in the end. It didn't. It was easy to see where I wanted to be going and I rather cockily thought that I could work my way back onto the route. I was just a couple of fields off, after all. But it appears that you can't get in and out of fields in the same way as you can streets. I have never got the hang of the whole 'right of way' thing, either, and what little I know of it leads me to believe that landowners resent them deeply. How much more would they resent someone trespassing and annoying the skittish sheep I was now traipsing among? I became increasingly nervous, seeing an irate farmer emerging from every culvert and copse, shotgun in hand, or else slackening his grip on some slavering, wild-eyed hound and shouting something incomprehensible in the local dialect. No doubt this was the sort of thing that Tolkien would have found infinitely absorbing.[3]

I jumped over a fence onto the main road and headed for the pub again to start over: not, of course, to drink, just to start over. I guessed that the first part of the route would be the one that Tolkien took between his lodgings and the village, given that the road between the two could hardly be more tangential. The second time round I found the right stile and suddenly the trail began to make some kind of sense. It takes you through a couple of kissing gates as you hold to the edge of Fox Fall Wood. A thin stream nestles between two shallow hills, but opens out into a pool close to your feet, long dark grasses – brown, beige and black – contrasting with the dry green of the surrounding fields.

Whatever you might wish to read into the landscape is diminished by the human elements. Between the Shireburn Arms and the school, for instance, there is a bright red-brick pavilion, jaunty enough to seem like something out of *Oh, What a Lovely War!*, despite the faded green of its paintwork. It belongs to a particular period in English history and a particular class too. Neither of them was inimical or unfamiliar to Tolkien, it is true, but the pavilion is nevertheless distracting. Matters aren't helped by the tractor standing idle beside the pavilion, blue as a child's plastic toy.

Further on is an observatory; the gate you pass through was once a dark turquoise but is now thick with rust. Swallows skid low above the cricket pitch, catching flies in the soft heat. I looked up at the vast squarish blank mass of the school, which is imposing and authoritative rather than aesthetically pleasing. The copper leaf on the cupolas that top its many towers is now mostly silver-grey, though some parts are still at least green. Smoke rose from a bonfire on the far side of Stonyhurst; crows swooped over fallow fields. Something is definitely wrong here, I thought: something is missing. It wasn't just the stillness. By now I could hear the distant buzz of the blue tractor, but in any case the green quiet here simply reflects the valley's status as a backwater. Even deep in the

English countryside it can sometimes be hard to escape the sound of traffic, whether the occasional roar of the passing car or the distant monotonous hiss of a motorway. But this hush must be what it was like for Tolkien in the petrol-rationed 1940s, with only the farm vehicles to remind one of the 20th century.

I went back to the observatory and sat on the verge. The hills on the horizon were now ghosting through the mist, although Pendle Hill itself was still a white space, a kind of cipher. I had to admit to myself that this felt strange: the one natural feature that dominates the country for miles around being swathed in cloud on a hot, increasingly clear summer's day. I won't say that it felt slightly mystical, because it didn't. But in its absence the hill bore down on the fields beneath as surely as it must when visible, casting a strange, notional shadow.

Pendle Hill does have a notoriety all of its own, and not just for its mists, although its association with bad weather certainly goes back a long way. Camden, for instance, writes:

> where [the] Ribble comes into Lancashire, Pendle Hill advanceth itself up to the sky, with a lofty head... But [it] is most notorious for the harm that it did long since to the country lying beneath it, by reason of a mighty deal of water gushing out of it; as also for an infallible prognostication of rain, so often as the top there is covered with a mist.

I have to confess that I get the kind of thrill reading this – a truth observable today in a book some 400 years old – that I think Tolkien got from, say, the word *Earendil*. It provides a sense of continuity, an immediacy born of recognition, that collapses the intervening centuries. (There's a lot of it to be had in Camden, who is an entertaining, informative and, for his day at least, reliable guide. This is Camden on Solihull, for instance: 'I saw Solyhill; but in it, setting aside the church, there is nothing worth sight.' For me, too, there is a physical pleasure in handling a book of that age, its heft, the dry smell of the discoloured pages, deciphering the marginalia for the stray and idle thoughts – the personal moments – of the long dead.) But whereas my delight projects forward, from the date of the book's first publication to the present day, Tolkien's delight projected backward, from *Earendil,* or *woses,* or *ent,* or *orthanc,* or *orc,* or any of the other curiosities he found in the first recorded English literature, into unremembered time.

However, Pendle Hill's lasting fame is primarily based on its associations with witchcraft. True, it is also associated with Quakerism: in 1652 George Fox, the founder of the Quakers, had a vision at the summit, in which God showed him all the places in England that would require his ministry, and he says in his autobiography that it marked the beginning of a new era. Clearly, as a devout Catholic Tolkien would not have had much time for someone like George Fox, but you would be hard-pressed to find a subject for which Tolkien would have had less sympathy than he had for witchcraft. Yet Tolkien was also highly rational. Neither Catholicism nor rationalism is particularly conducive to an interest in black magic. But still, for all the absence of religion and cults – and worship generally – from his fiction, there are unnamed evil things in the dark corners of the land that owe nothing to Sauron.

Tolkien was also susceptible to the idea that evil can leave its impress on a landscape long after its possessors have themselves passed away. It's not an uncommon perception of Pendle Hill. People talk about its heritage as if there were a continuity, rather than a single incident.

The story, set in the early years of the reign of James I (James VI of Scotland) – a fervent believer in witchcraft and demonology – is briefly this. A woman by the name of Alizon Device was refused the purchase of some pins by a beggar. He collapsed shortly afterwards and his son accused Alizon of having cursed him. Perhaps surprisingly, she confessed, but in so doing she incriminated a number of other women, who in turn incriminated others. Most of them belonged to three local families, the Chattos, the Demdikes and the Devices, between whom there had been a long-standing feud. Ultimately a total of 20 people were accused of crimes ranging from bewitching cattle and charming milk into butter to 17 counts of murder. Mostly the latter were based on confessions of curses laid before the victims' deaths, but Elizabeth Demdike, Alizon's grandmother, did explain another method to her inquisitors, which seems to have been a kind of voodoo:

> The speediest way to take a man's life away by witchcraft is to make a picture of clay, like unto the shape of the person whom they meane to kill, and dry it thoroughly: and when they would have them to be ill in any one place more than another; then take a thorn or pin, and price it in that part of the picture you would so have to be ill: and when you would have any part of the body to consume away, then take that part of the picture, and

burn it. And when they would have the whole body to
consume away, then take the remnant of the said picture,
and burn it: and so thereupon by that means, the body
shall die.[4]

It is a strange story, not least because the witches – not exclusively women – wilfully incriminated close relatives as well as
themselves before the trial started. There may have been some
degree of coercion, although torture was forbidden in English
witch trials, in contradistinction to Scotland and continental
Europe. Perhaps that was how they saw themselves: some human
teeth and a clay image were found at Elizabeth Demdike's house,
where, it was said, a witches' sabbath had been held on Good
Friday. But they also went so far as to confess to selling their souls
to familiar demons, sometimes in human form, but also in the
guise of a black dog or bull. (They were trumped in the self-
delusion stakes by one John Palmer, who at his trial in 1649
claimed to have turned himself into a toad, the better to pursue
his victim.) The outcome of the Pendle trial was probably a fore-
gone conclusion, given the scale of the confessions, but not wholly
so. Not all the accused were found guilty; one defendant,
Margaret Pearson, was found guilty of witchcraft, but not of murder, and was sentenced to a year's imprisonment. Ten of them,
however, were hanged at Lancaster Gaol on 20th August 1612.

Witchcraft itself, as it is popularly understood, is a relatively
recent idea. Until the late Middle Ages it simply didn't have the
exclusive connotation of Devil worship. Its wholesale association
with evil is a post-Reformation development, part of the gradual
draining away of the supernatural from anything beyond the Holy

Trinity, a process that had already begun in pre-Reformation Catholicism. 'The medieval church,' writes Keith Thomas in *Religion and the Decline of Magic*, 'appeared as a vast reservoir of magical powers, capable of being deployed for a variety of secular purposes.' Before the Reformation in England votive offerings and prayers to popular saints did not differ wildly from those offered to Nodens at Lydney (see Chapter 3). The recitation of the mass could be enough to ward off evil, to counter the effect of a curse that relied on the same magic: the power of the spoken word to effect material change. Candles were lit to ensure the safety of those going on long journeys; communion silver could be carried as a lucky charm; holy water was sprinkled on barren ground to make it fertile; prayers could be recited backwards to render them malevolent. Even Anglo-Saxon charters (such as those referred to, in relation to the Berkshire Downs, in Chapter 8) were attached to church altars or copied into holy books to underline the formidable consequences of breaking faith.

However, the church did not have a monopoly on popular magic, and it seemed happy to co-exist with other forms, albeit more tacitly than anything else. As Professor Thomas points out:

> There were many pagan survivals – magic wells, calendar customs, fertility rites – just as there were many types of magical activity. But these practices did not usually involve any formal breach with Christianity, and were, as often as not, followed by men and women who would have indignantly repudiated any aspersions on their religious faith.[5]

People were as likely to go to a local cunning man or wise woman as an apothecary or a physician for any healing they required. Given the state of medical knowledge, they were probably not any the worse for it. Even for those who practised maleficent magic, however, there was little interest in legal sanctions. Records are inevitably patchy in their survival and therefore inconclusive, but it may be that as few as six witches were executed between the Norman Conquest and the English Reformation, and they were typically involved in plots against the crown or ruling clique.

As for Tolkien, he clearly accepted, as evidenced by what Galadriel says about her mirror, that there were different kinds of magic, and that the same word could be applied to her as to Sauron, whose first appearance in print was as the Necromancer in *The Hobbit.* To that extent Tolkien aligns himself with the older tradition, as you might expect. Indeed, the fact that he felt it necessary to spell out the difference between Galadriel's ability to scry the future, however conditionally, and the inventions of Sauron suggests that it was an issue that he felt to be of some sensitivity. But there are other kinds of 'good' magic in Middle Earth, from the power channelled through Gandalf's staff to Aragorn's ability to heal with the herb *athelas.* Tolkien may not have been interested in the belief systems associated with magic, but he was certainly moved by the notion of ideas surviving in oral traditions, corrupted, yet offering echoes of true things, and displaying continuities despite subjugation and cultural loss. In his essay 'On Fairy Stories' he discusses briefly the misuse of the word 'magic', or at least its blanket use for a wide range of phenomena. Magic, he says, is what magicians do; the rest is art.[6]

Back on the verge by the observatory, I had found what was troubling me: the landscape is dominated by Stonyhurst. Grand though it is, it represents a period and a style wholly out of keeping with any notions one might have of the Shire, never mind Middle Earth in general. Despite the evident wealth of its owners, it was built after the period in which the rich felt the need to fortify their homes with any degree of seriousness. At its heart it is a country house on a gargantuan scale. While you can reconcile smaller such properties with the Shire, this is more in keeping with an 18th-century novel. No one but an Englishman of prodigious income and a certain standing could ever live here. It offers another layer of England to consider, but it is one that Tolkien's sensibility had little affection for; he had trouble, after all, communicating an interest in much literature later than Geoffrey Chaucer. If it is a challenge to imagine hobbits on the Berkshire Downs (see Chapter 8), it is close to impossible here.

Nevertheless, I pressed on. If nothing else, there was shade up ahead in Over Hacking Wood. The path here takes you steeply downhill, to two bridges across shallow, rocky streams, before rising again towards Hodder Place, a late 18th-century cotton-mill-owner's house high above the River Hodder. The shade is cool and soft on the eye, and the many pine trees in the sparse woodland mean that the sun fleetingly breaks through the green roof, feathering the coffee-toned hillside with a golden light. There are roots aplenty twisted underfoot, which more careful feet than mine would still stumble over; a foot or so to the left the path falls sharply away. Some day someone concerned with health and safety will put some rails here. I was reminded of Box Hill in Surrey, where, in the glorious spirit of English eccentricity bordering on mania, a Major Peter Labelliere was buried upside down in 1800, having stipulated in his will that first the youngest son and daughter of his landlady should dance on his coffin.

I stopped outside the walls of Hodder Place and listened to the rush of the river far below. The trees are particularly thin here on the steep bank, which, I imagine, is too sheer to hold the weight of many of them. Stepping close to the edge, I could glimpse the water pushing fast over the rocks in the river's shallow bed. Across the river and beyond the trees are green fields rising to the horizon. Further downstream the Hodder rolls over a weir like molten metal into the hissing foam below. That there is also a weir in the Withywindle is most likely to be a coincidence.

After the weir, the river calms, so much so that, when I saw it, this stretch of the Hodder was studded with families picnicking on its sunbathed banks and swimming carelessly as the river curves to the south. I could hear nothing but children splashing and shouting with considerable zeal. I remembered that the River Ribble, shortly to join the Hodder, is, like so many English rivers, presided over by a malevolent female spirit, or hag, called Peg O'Nell, who demanded animal sacrifices every seven years if children were to remain safe on her banks. It must, I thought wistfully, be somewhat more than seven years since she were last placated. (Lancashire is also home to the more unpleasant Jenny Greenteeth, who lives in stagnant pools, where she will steal any child who strays too close.) Goldberry, when we first meet her in 'The Adventures of Tom Bombadil', seems to be a sanitized version of these hags, pulling Tom down beneath the water as a river-woman's daughter should. Her mother, in her deep weed-choked pool, might be more like Peg O'Nell.

I looked again at the water flowing past, shallow in the summer heat, antique gold in the sun. All around, meanwhile, the hills and ridges paled into pure distance, into the white of a horizon that barely turned blue before the clear sun, high in the sky to the south, forced my gaze away. Woodland sat like low-rolling cloud on the brow of the hills. Butterflies dodged and burned in the bright light along the path. This was a good place to be on a summer's day in northern England, but I felt as if Tolkien was receding into the background as the day's drowsy warmth washed over me. I hadn't thought it before, but in some sense my idea of the Shire is yoked to temperate weather: somewhere that is rainy, inclined to chill, huddled under grey skies close to the sodden earth.

I pushed on to Hacking Hall, which stands on the further bank – high, sandy and burrowed – just after the Hodder has been joined from the east by the River Calder. Boulders break the water here like fallen horses, the sunlight rippling silver on its dark surface like some kind of a slipstream. If you are starting from the idea that the map of the Shire may be congruent with that of the valley, then Hacking Hall is in the wrong place if it is supposed, as it often is, to be Brandy Hall. Moreover, Brandy Hall must be a much more expansive place, since, according to Tolkien, it has three main doors and more than 100 windows (although when it first appeared in draft it claimed a mere 50 windows, which isn't that many; my own home, a three-bedroom house in a terrace, can summon up 11). Hacking Hall is more modest than Brandy Hall, being a large Jacobean place, the sheep scattering across the fields before it: suitable for a gentleman, perhaps, but not for a lord.

I was surprised by my reaction. Identifying and visiting Tom Bombadil's cottage had left me feeling a little deflated, almost disappointed, despite the incontrovertible evidence in support of the identification. Here, where the evidence is thin, I felt a real sense of elation. I realized that it wasn't certainty that I was seeking, after all; that would be too reductive. What I wanted was possibility only, no more than a good chance, something that still allowed room for interpretation, speculation and wonder.

Hacking Hall, for instance, shares with Brandy Hall its location on a strip of land on the far side of a river before woods rise up behind it. For hobbits from elsewhere in the Shire, Buckland's location already represents a step away from safety, having been established to the east of the Brandywine, which had originally provided a natural boundary. In *The Lord of the Rings* Bucklanders are regarded as different, almost alien, and certainly peculiar for wanting to live where they do. There might be an echo here of the deep and historic distrust between the neighbouring counties of Lancashire and Yorkshire: I say distrust, but that's really too simple a word to convey the profundity of their rancour, which dates from the Wars of the Roses, when their respective lords fought over the English throne. Earlier, when Jonathan had mentioned the Pendle witches to me, he had said, more or less as an afterthought, 'Of course, it is Yorkshire on the other side', as if that explained everything, satanic practices included; and he, after all, is only an adopted Lancastrian. These rivalries are still in the air.

When I discovered that the River Hodder marked the ancient border between the two counties I began to think that this might be Buckland after all.

There is also a ferry a few yards upstream, or, to be more accurate, there was a ferry. It was dismantled in the 1950s and now lives a shrunken life in nearby Clitheroe Museum, together, somewhat forlornly, with the ferryman's hut. The ferry was certainly still carrying passengers across the still narrow stretch of water when Tolkien visited the valley in the early 1940s, before road traffic became quite so overwhelmingly popular. The house and the ferry are closer together than Brandy Hall and Bucklebury are in the novel, but the coincidence is a striking one, and, perhaps perversely, I am inclined to find it more compelling than Tolkien's drawing of Tom Bombadil's house.

Chapter Seven
Cheddar Gorge, Somerset; Brill, Buckinghamshire

One thing that marks the England that Tolkien knew from the England that we might visit now is that the success of his work has made him attractive to the tourism and leisure industry. In other words, Tolkien himself increasingly figures in the landscape. In some cases this is a benign development. There are plans, for instance, to build a Tolkien Park in the Sarehole area (see Chapter 5), which would encompass both the mill and Moseley Bog, and contain facilities to enable the study of Tolkien, as well as those more suited to a family attraction. Other cases are more ambivalent: Jonathan Hewat told me that he was once approached by a company looking to create some kind of Tolkien-related theme park in the Ribble Valley (see Chapter 6). It is surely only a matter of time before there is a Tolkien theme park somewhere in Britain. Could anyone resist a ride through the Mines of Moria? I doubt it.

Meanwhile, there is a particularly egregious example of the

trend at the caves of the Cheddar Gorge in Somerset, a dozen or so miles southwest of Bristol. Two caves in the gorge are open to the public: Gough's Cave and Cox's Cave. The latter is the more modest of the two, both in extent and in spectacle, which is perhaps why it has developed an entertainment called the Crystal Quest, running through a number of the caverns. It enables the owners to use various sound and lighting effects, including the kind of spinning spotlights more often seen in discos and nightclubs, to inject some drama into the otherwise quite muted proceedings. I say drama, but that is perhaps an overstatement. I couldn't catch every word of the narrative voicetrack. It was rather muffled, although I'm not sure whether that was due to poor reproduction or simply to the imperfect acoustics of the caves. It featured the usual motley post-Tolkien fantasy ensemble of knights and wizards (one good and one bad from what I could tell), as well as a dragon, breathing dry ice, on guard over the crystal. The presence of wraiths was revealing, since they are a very Tolkienish invention, as was a reference to elves that clearly envisaged them as they are in his Middle Earth, rather than as the diminutive and mischievous fairies that appear in, for instance, *A Midsummer Night's Dream*. Someone or something on the dark side, if I can use the phrase, was also called Mordor. Actually, with allowances for the challenging sound quality, it could well have been a name that merely recalled 'Mordor'. (At times I thought it was Morden, best-known to Londoners as the southernmost stop on the Northern Line of the Underground, but that seemed an implausible choice.)

It's not a big project, encompassing only two or three corridors and one largeish chamber, but its capacity to make the heart sink was overwhelming. I appreciate that, at 37, I am probably some 30 years outside the target demographic, although the day I was there visiting children seemed divided between indifference and mild terror. The fact that you have to save the world yourself by touching the 'crystal' in the centre of the chamber – which I thought was a nice element of interactivity – appeared to provoke trepidation and disbelief in the children, and it was mostly the parents, self-consciously shuffling forward with embarrassment, who did it on their behalf.

There's nothing inherently wrong with this kind of attraction, or for that matter with borrowing elements here and there from Tolkien's mythology, full as it is of widespread borrowings of its own. But the extraordinary ubiquity of Tolkien and Tolkien-derived fantasy can obscure the unrivalled richness and depth of his creation, smoothing out its gnarled complexities and rendering his books down into a contemporary cartoonish idiom, perfectly fine in itself, but wholly antithetical to the rescue and celebration of antiquity that is at the heart of his work. At Cox's cave, in particular, the display diminishes the work it refers to, while also turning a phenomenon of some natural beauty into a plastic and more or less irrelevant backdrop. Tolkien visited Cheddar in 1940 and apparently thought that it was too heavily commercialized even then.[1] My head spins wondering what he would think of it now.

It is particularly galling in any case, since there is a rare cast-iron link between the caves here and the landscape of *The Lord of the Rings*. They offer one of the few instances where Tolkien made explicit the relationship between a real place and his act of 'sub-creation': he admitted to a correspondent that the Cheddar caves were the model for the caverns at Helm's Deep and perhaps, more specifically, for Gimli's enraptured description of them to Legolas on the road to Isengard. It's an impassioned speech, full of love for both the place itself in its natural state and what it could become under the shaping hand of the craftsman. The question is whether the reality has anything to tell us about the use that Tolkien made of it.

According to Christopher Tolkien, when his father first conceived Helm's Deep he played around with a number of possible names, among them 'Heorulf's Clough', 'the Dimhale' and 'the Long Clough'. 'Clough' is derived from an Anglo-Saxon word meaning 'steep-sided valley', 'hale' from a word meaning 'corner of land'. Tolkien also toyed in the margins of his draft of *The Lord of the Rings* with words meaning 'narrow place' and 'deep profound'.[2] Cumulatively they convey a good sense of what the gorge at Cheddar is like. It's a defile to the east of the village of the same name, trees rooted precariously on the almost sheer grey rock walls on either side, which reach up several hundred feet above the black snake of the road winding its way up out of the gorge. Inside there's an eerie sense of pressure, as if you're standing in the grip of a slowly closing vice. If you look up, you feel that the lips of the valley could almost be drawing together, shutting out the sky and the world beyond the rocks' edge. Perhaps this embrace should generate a sense of security, but I felt little more than disquiet, despite the Romantic allure of the rugged wilderness, which, tamed though it is by centuries of English domestication, can still tug at the imagination.

Cheddar Gorge is a good place to visit if you want to comprehend why ancient peoples built their settlements on hill-tops. That is why it is ironic that the caves here should have been appropriated to fill the interior of Helm's Deep, a wholly defensive position. These seemed to me to be strange thoughts to find myself thinking, but the kind of awe that the gorge inspires isn't entirely free from a sense of the danger and brutal dread of nature too. It is magical: I can clearly remember coming here as a child and then dreaming about this wild, ruined cleft in the Earth's crust, the sky above cropped to a narrow misshapen strip. But it is at heart inhospitable.

The caves here weren't discovered until the very end of the 19th century, by people who made a living by turning them into entertainment. My childhood memory of Gough's cave, the more extraordinary of the two by some margin, is one of rapt wonder. Gimli articulates the feeling well. For people who, like me, are more used to thinking of caves as angular, human things, hewn out of the rock by axe and hammer, the fluidity of the stone here is a revelation, having a delicacy and grace that seems almost supernatural, and certainly not of our craft. I remember deep caverns, their far walls obscurely lit and wrapped in shadow; high-vaulted chambers, the walls of which were like the melted pipes of some vast stone church organ, picked out in soft pinks and greens and yellows; and perfect, clear rock pools, magnifying the mountainous ceilings. Everything gleamed wet in the bright lights.

Visiting again, I was surprised by how much I remembered; and it was all radiant still, brilliant. Yet after Gimli it seems a modest thing indeed, shrunk from the great underground city that he promises to a mere handful of rooms. I was much more aware now of the degree to which perceptions are manipulated by the dramatic lighting in the cave. The mirror pools that had seemed lucid and beautiful appeared no more than an effect, there to bounce more light around the chambers and to save the tourists from the bother of raising their eyes upwards. In a way, the fact that we know of a direct correlation with a place in *The Lord of the Rings* serves to diminish the work a little. What could have been described as an act of imaginative translation now seemed to hover perilously close to plain exaggeration. Holding the knowledge of the two places in one's head did little to illuminate the caves of Aglarond: Cheddar seems less transformed than inflated, so that its features seem somewhat blurred, almost bloated.

I came to the conclusion that Tolkien was right to be wary about conceding such points about the relation between real places and his imaginary ones, since it is the ambiguity of his world's relationship to England that generates meaning, not its explicitness. He had tried the more direct approach with *The Book of Lost Tales* and other unfinished works, and he had failed. He was right to avoid revealing his sources for another reason too. It's a statement of the obvious, but Tolkien wrote epic fantasy – or, if you prefer, heroic romance – for which a sense of wonder is a prerequisite. Hyperbole had to be part of his stock in trade. It may have been one of his great creative leaps to introduce into his landscape the prosaic and down-to-earth hobbits, whose native caution and restraint serve as much-needed correctives to some of the more elaborate scenes in the books. But that elaboration is a necessary condition of the genre: in the context of his invention, where, disbelief suspended, many curiosities escape questioning, the kind of speech he gives to Gimli functions perfectly.

Nevertheless, it is something of a relief that most of the correspondences one might deduce are less straightforward and therefore offer less scope for disappointment. Tolkien's England as it emerged into print is a fragmentary, allusive thing. However attractive an idea it is to map possible derivations exactly onto Middle Earth, the reality is more slippery and more difficult. Part of this is due simply to the scale of Tolkien's work and the complex process of translation that any possible sources might go through before they were fixed in *The Lord of the Rings* or elsewhere.

To an extent, I mean that literally. Tolkien's construction of Elvish place names, for instance, out of the same basic units of meaning as any in the real world, and mostly derived therefore from elements of landscape, leaves us with impossibly rudimentary descriptions as our starting points. Take 'Imladris': Tolkien was particularly pleased with his translation of this word into 'Rivendell' since the match is exact, but with that fact alone to work with the prospect of identifying the place that inspired him to create it is a remote one.

Even where the sources are apparent, sorting through the layers of usage – of history, culture and language – and sifting significance from what is physically evident in England now can lead one to be too emphatic, to overstate the truth, placing too much stress on connections that in fact are mostly tangential and allusive. A case in point might be Bree, which is widely regarded as being based on Brill in Buckinghamshire, a few miles to the northeast of Oxford.[3]

That Tolkien knew Brill is unarguable. His children, discussing their father with the biographer Humphrey Carpenter, recalled autumnal trips out to villages such as Brill and nearby Worminghall as part of the family's shared pleasure in storytelling and in the sense of place. Tolkien put some of this to good use in *Farmer Giles of Ham* (a story that isn't set in Middle Earth), in which this small quiet corner of country is transformed into the Little Kingdom. Worminghall, Thame and Oakley all feature explicitly in the story, Thame being the Ham of the title; Rollright is there, too, if unnamed.[4] The specificity of these references was clearly a matter of importance to Tolkien, since he got quite irate with an illustrator who overlooked it.

But what elements of Brill did he borrow? First, of course, there was a degree of inspiration in the name. The name 'Brill' is a contraction of 'bree hill', derived from the Celtic word *bre*, meaning 'hill', and the Anglo-Saxon word *hyll*, also meaning, as is probably evident, 'hill'. Thus 'Brill' means 'hill hill'. Historians take this kind of synthesis as demonstrating the supplanting, rather than the assimilation, of one language group by another. The model underlying this conclusion is that the incoming people heard the defeated natives using the name but, not understanding its meaning – because, it is assumed, the two language groups did not cohabit to any degree – added their own element to clarify for themselves what was meant. (The process has been taken one step further in Cornwall, where there is a Brill Hill – 'hill hill hill' – just north of the Helford Estuary on the Lizard peninsula.) As noted elsewhere (in Chapter 4), Tolkien deliberately gave the area around Bree names with at least one foot in Welsh. You can see several of them in the area around Brill: Chetwode is to the north and Coombe to the west, over the Oxfordshire border.

The historical record bears out the extent to which Brill, or the site of it, like most of southern central England, has been under many dominions. There is evidence of an Iron Age hill fort beneath the village. Like Bree itself, Brill has an ancient road running not many miles away. Here it is the great Roman road from Cirencester to St Albans, now known as Akeman Street, which may itself be in part built on a more prehistoric route. Tom Shippey argues that a poem by Tolkien's friend G.B. Smith about a Roman road across the downs must refer to Akeman Street. Memory of the Roman colonization of Britain faded quickly and the Saxons came to look on these structures, with their straight lines scythed imperially through the landscape, as strange marvels, '*orthanc enta geweorc*', 'the skilful work of giants' (Tolkien's creation of the Ents from this phrase is distinctively his own). Later the kings of Wessex made Brill into a royal manor. A Saxon castle survived from the seventh century to the 14th and its defences, ironically, were strengthened a few years before the Norman Conquest.

As Tolkien said, most likely with a hint of regret, of the woodland outside Bree, the land around Brill was tamed long ago. The road into the village from the southeast is tidily hedged, and the fields are low and even: only the occasional yew or oak erupts to break the comfortable perspective. The towns and villages along the way, such as Thame and Long Crendon, display a very English mixture of styles, the more prosperous 18th- and 19th-century red-brick premises jostling for space beside brightly painted terraces with absurdly low ceilings and half-timbered Tudor houses rendered with unpainted lime or the more usual white plaster. One cottage, the drop of its gables almost reaching to the ground, is swathed in wisteria, its boughs coiling up like smooth, silver green ropes beside the front door.

Brill itself is more expansive, if probably less peopled. There is a wide green and another civic space further along, with the war memorials typical of many English villages recording the names of the fallen, the length of the lists without exception revealing the heartbreaking scale of loss. Some 28 families in Brill lost members in the Great War, for instance; one, the Claridges, had four young men to mourn.

Brill is also less pretty than some of the neighbouring villages. I did experience a flutter of excitement when I saw a gate beside one of the roads into Brill, but in truth that is by no means uncommon in this area and its function is little more than decorative now, if it was ever anything more. Indeed, it is not much more than a farm gate to look at, painted a gleaming white, for all the world like something from a model railway. The step from this to the gate at Bree is a large one: it seems inconceivable to me that Tolkien could have got to the great gate in the hedge from what's on offer in Brill. There is also at least one pub, the Red Lion, in an odd, low hexagonal building where, if you come from the north, the road indeed sweeps round to the right past the village green. It's possible that this inspired the Prancing Pony, but on the whole I think it is unlikely. One of the latter's distinguishing features is that it was built to cater for a greater volume of traffic along the roads than it is receiving at the time when Frodo and his companions sup there. I would hazard a guess that if the Red Lion was suffering the same kind of shortfall custom would have to be thin indeed. It is small enough to seem busy with only a handful of customers.

What does mark the village out is its setting: the hill. It crops up in a nursery rhyme: 'Brill on the hill where the wind blows shrill'.[5] To the east it sits almost on an escarpment, overlooking the flat lands below and barely troubled by the low hills looming gently out of the plain. By the time I reached Brill summer had mostly gone and, despite the warmth left in the sun, the wind seemed almost brittle, with something piercing and harsh riding in across the featureless landscape of East Anglia from the North Sea and beyond. White houses with slate roofs nestled in culverts, burrowed down against the approaching frosts; the huddled groves were full of birdsong. The fields were wide and modern, but still pleasingly asymmetrical, irregular, still clinging a little to the contours of the land.

I think you can glimpse Bree, or a ghost of it, in some of the features of Brill. There are too many layers of meaning and attribution to be emphatic, but on one of those levels at least the Shire is a shadow of Oxfordshire. Tolkien stated to one correspondent that he had deliberately placed Hobbiton and Rivendell at approximately the same latitude as Oxford, with all that followed about the relative geographical positions of Minas Tirith and so on also being intentional.[6] Brill, a little way over the county boundary from Oxfordshire, looks nervously to the east, from where the darkness comes.

From all this the significance of place names shines through.

They can tell us a vast amount about the beliefs, history and identity of a people. Indeed, the earlier you step back into English history, the more vital to the historian they become. We know almost
nothing about Celtic England except as it was encountered and
defeated by the Romans, and thereby brought into their history.
Of its engagements with the Anglo-Saxon invaders of the fifth
century onwards there is little or no direct testimony. Among the
things we do have are place names. They can be used to illustrate
people's engagement with one another – the clash of civilizations,
if you like – as well as their engagement with the landscape. As
with Brill, names can reveal shifts in political power. It is sobering
to reflect that, as noted by Margaret Melling in her three-volume
Place Names of Berkshire, a mere 18 of those names actually contain any pre-English elements, among them river names such as
'Thames' and 'Severn'. We simply don't know whether this reflects
Saxon subjugation, Celtic accommodation or, indeed, enforced
migration or worse. Melling comments, bleakly: 'we should seek a
term other than continuity, which, however modified, implies
survival'.[7]

Naturally, there are numerous theories about understanding
place names and what may reasonably be inferred from that
understanding. One that has some currency argues that place
names that are descriptive of landscapes necessarily pre-date those
that require some kind of social development. Hence, with regard
to Anglo-Saxon, names with elements such as *hamm* ('land in a
river bend, promontory'), *haga* ('hedge, enclosure'), *graf* ('grove,
copse') or *stan* ('stone') are probably older than those with, say, *tun*
('enclosure, farmstead, village') or *weg* ('way, road') in them. As in

Berkshire, the names of major rivers, as fixed landmarks, are among those most likely to endure with little or no change, and to skip from one language group to its successor.

One of the particular fascinations of this approach to history is that it reflects the actions of people who work on the land on a daily basis. Such shifts as take place are not top down, the results of the fiats of an elite. To quote Melling again:

> Neither the Roman occupation of the 1st century AD, which brought a Latin-speaking administration close to Britain, nor the Norman Conquest of 1066, which brought a new French-speaking aristocracy, caused a major replacement of the pre-existing place names by new place names in the language of the conquerors. It seems likely that a replacement of the kind which happened at the end of the Roman period…occurs only when the newcomers are farmers rather than, or as well as, overlords.

The image that this conjures up, of people negotiating over every stone of land, every ditch and post and pit and hollow, the things of boundary marks and charters, each one a little victory or defeat, is rather a moving one.

Chapter Eight
The Berkshire Downs

If there is one place that belongs to Tolkien's England it is the Berkshire Downs. He first visited them in 1912, at the end of his first year at university, traipsing across the countryside and drawing the villages. Although Swindon is the nearest town, Oxford isn't far, perhaps 25 miles to the northeast. Later in life Tolkien took his children on walks across the downs, climbing White Horse Hill and exploring Wayland's Smithy, and recounting to them some of the stories that had risen from the landscape.

They are not extensive, these hills, which are bordered to the north and east by the Thames, to the south by the Vale of Kennet, and to the west by the Avon Vale. Nor are they dramatic in the way that, say, the Derbyshire Peak District or the Cumbrian Lakes are. Wild romanticism plays little part in their character. The landscape of the Downs is, rather, fluid and reserved. Yet Tolkien, I think, wished to see it otherwise: not wild itself, but with wild things in it, with a long cold history that underlies its civility and rises up beneath it like shadows in the fog.

We'll come to the barrows later. The better-known monument

on the downs is the White Horse of Uffington, cut into a typically chalky hillside between Swindon and Wantage. Unlike almost all of the other white horses cut into hills in southern England, this one is genuinely very old. Most of the others do not appear in the records until the last few hundred years, certainly well into the modern era; evidence for the horse at Uffington reaches back to the 11th century and there's no particular reason to suppose that it was new, then. Indeed, quite the opposite. Naturally there has been some disagreement about its origins. The two basic theories have it as either Saxon or Celtic.

According to the former theory it was cut by King Alfred the Great to commemorate his victory over the Danes at nearby Ashdown in 871, a white horse being the emblem carried on Saxon war banners. In some versions the barrow at Wayland's Smithy, a mile or so down the Ridgeway, becomes the burial mound of the Danish king. One problem this theory presents is that the actual site of the battle remains unknown, Ashdown being an Old English name for the downs as a whole. Speculation seems to point to its being sited near to East Ilsley, some way to the east of Uffington and the Vale of the White Horse. Another problem is that Wayland's Smithy predates Alfred by some 3,000 years.

The other theory, which is the more generally accepted one, is that the horse is Celtic, not least because of the strong similarity between its design and that of the horses to be found on coins of the local Belgic people. In fact, it probably dates from between 100 BC and 100 AD, although some would push that first date back as far as 1000 BC.[1]

It's worth mentioning, however, that there is also a tradition that the horse was cut by Hengist, the legendary fifth-century warrior who became co-founder of England alongside his brother Horsa. Both men find their way explicitly into *The Book of Lost Tales* as the sons of Eriol, born before he sailed west to Tol Eressëa. They find echoes, too, in *The Lord of the Rings*, where Tolkien makes his story of the founding of the Shire mirror theirs. For example, Hengist and Horsa are both words for horses. The same is true, albeit obscurely, of the names that Tolkien gives to the founders of the Shire: Marcho and Blanco. The latter means 'white horse'.[2]

Whatever the practice in ancient times, into the modern era there was a festival every seven years called, accurately enough, the Scouring of the White Horse, during which it was cleaned. Thomas Baskerville, in the journal of his travels in 1667–8, wrote of it that:

> Some that dwell hereabout have an obligation upon their lands to reopen and cleanse this land mark; or else in time it may turn green like the rest of the hill, and be forgotten.

I had always thought of 'The Scouring of the Shire' in *The Lord of the Rings* as referring to a process of cleansing, but perhaps it echoes this event, too, as a celebration and reaffirmation of identity and character. Certainly the people of the area regarded it as an occasion for pleasure: as many as 30,000 of them turned out to enjoy the festivities the last time they were on offer, on Whit Monday 1857. Games included rolling a cheese down the hill, wrestling, mock sword fights and other amusements. The site is now maintained by English Heritage, which doesn't go in for that sort of thing in quite the same way.

In some ways I contrived to visit the Downs on a typical English summer's day. By the time I arrived it was warming up, but driving from London I'd got caught in a tremendous rainstorm that slowed the traffic on the motorway to a suburban crawl, as cars even 30 feet in front became invisible through the fog of rain, lights or no lights. After I'd turned off onto the side roads past Woodland St Mary and Lambourn, the weather lifted a little and the road itself began to ride up, bucking and pitching through the hedged fields, as sunlight broke through the green trees and shadows littered the tarmac, still bloated in places with the morning's rain.

At Uffington it's a brisk walk up the hill from the car park, across a field liberally fertilized by the sheep grazing in it. It's a strange sensation approaching a monument that you struggle to see from the ground. I was sure I was heading in the right direction only because there were a few huddles of tourists like myself in one particular spot. Most were there for the same reason as me, although one 20-something man had chosen the site to play with his remote-controlled plane, which whirred like a bee in an upturned cup as it skimmed the hillside above the horse, riding the blustery warm north wind.

The horse itself, viewed from afar, is a spare, elegant object, nearly 400 feet long, with great grace and vigour in its lithe, muscular movement. Standing close by offers a different sensation, since you can't accommodate it all. The scoured hillside seems more disjointed, more abstract. There is a magnificent view, however, with Tolkien's Mercian heartlands of Oxfordshire and the

West Midlands laid out before you like a map. Who knows what the intention was of those who made the horse? Yet it is hard to believe that it wasn't some kind of statement of ownership and belonging. Whether that was a defiant one, or an emphatic expression of power and subjugation, akin to the vast statues of Lenin and his heirs that used to stand across central and eastern Europe, is open to question.

In a way it's a shame that the Saxon theory is the more discredited, or at least the more disavowed, of the two main contenders. When you're beside the horse it's easy to imagine that it lies, not on a hillside, but on a vast green banner unfurling in the wild wind. Perhaps that's something Tolkien sought to rectify, since that is precisely what the banner of Rohan depicts: a white horse on a green field. It is certainly not a coincidence. The men and women of the Mark have to all intents and purposes ridden straight out of Saxon England. Their names and language are Old English, as exemplified in the names of the kings, all of which are Old English words for 'king', save the first, 'Eorl', which means 'earl' or 'warrior'. In addition, the Rohirrim bury their dead in barrows; and the Rohirric poem that Aragorn recalls borrows more or less directly from the Anglo-Saxon poem *The Wanderer*, which, like *The Seafarer* (see Chapter 4), is a bitter lament of exile and loss, its poignancy heightened in an oral, memorializing culture for which death and defeat meant oblivion.

However, as Shippey has pointed out, Rohan is not merely Anglo-Saxon in some general sense, it is specifically Mercian. Its very name for itself, 'the Mark', is an attempt to recreate how its people might have referred to it, an act of rescue reclaiming it from Latinity and the victor's history. Rohan's language, or rather Tolkien's representation of it, conforms not to the Anglo-Saxon of Wessex but to that of Mercia.[3]

This kind of detail may at first sight seem a needless obscurity on Tolkien's part, a symptom of the kind of niggling that made it so difficult for him to finish his work. But surely it reflects his profound love for this particular area of England. If the Rohirrim are a clue, Tolkien's letters are more revealing. Of course, as with any volume of correspondence where readers have no personal knowledge of either writer or recipient, it isn't always easy to know when Tolkien is being facetious, or pursuing a little in-joke. Yet a point he makes on several occasions concerns the powerful affinity he felt for the West Midlands in general and, by extension, the ancient Saxon kingdom of Mercia, in particular.

Mercia is little regarded today. Aside from a few institutional names – the West Mercia Police Service, Mercia Sound, a local radio station based in Coventry, and so on – it is all but invisible. (I was intrigued to discover the existence of The Mercia Movement, a broadly left-wing political group, albeit marginal, which campaigns for Mercian devolution, if not secession, from the British state. Its programme is based on what it regards as a return to the values, laws and social structures of England before the Norman Conquest.) Mercia's existence was limited to the period between the seventh century and the early part of the 10th, by which time it was subject to the authority of its arch-enemy Wessex. Its heart was very much in what we call today the West Midlands: Mercia was formed by the amalgamation of two Germanic tribes, the Mierce around the Trent (actually descended from the Angles) and the Hwiccans in what is now Worcestershire. The name 'Mierce' means 'people of the march (border)', although it isn't known what border that refers to. At its apogee, under the eighth-century rule of Offa, who made his capital at Tamworth in Staffordshire, 20-odd miles southeast of Great Haywood, Mercia took in most of England south of the Humber and part of Wales too. Our lack of detailed knowledge about Mercia shouldn't be taken to mean that it was unimportant. At one point it was a major European power. In 789 Offa was important enough for Charlemagne to consider making a strategic alliance with him, through the marriage of his son Charles to one of Offa's daughters. Mercia's borders were constantly fought over and therefore constantly shifting, especially its border with Wessex, which for the most part hovered uneasily around the Berkshire Downs. The point where I stood beside the White Horse could well be taken to represent the threshold of Mercia, a restless frontier with a familial enemy.

That Wessex is the Anglo-Saxon kingdom we are most familiar with is at least in part due to the fact that the key historical text of the period, the *Anglo-Saxon Chronicle*, was a West Saxon, that is Wessex, document. (It is of course also due to its ultimate achievement of supremacy over the rival English kingdoms by the end of the 10th century.) Very little is known about Mercia and even that is largely the evidence of its enemies: the very name by which we know it is a latinization, after all. Culturally there are little more than hints. It has been suggested, for instance, that the way in which the unknown author of *Beowulf* went out of his way to praise Offa of Angeln, the putative forefather of the Mercian king, reflects a connection with the Mercian court. The same is said to be true of another Old English poem, *Widsith*, which also includes a line referring to 'Wade of the Helsingas' that Tolkien incorporated into an early, now fragmentary alliterative poem, the *Lay of Earendil*.[4]

Tolkien seems to have regarded Mercia almost as his cultural birthright, something he drew from his mother's lineage rather than his father's. He explained to his American publishers, for instance, that he believed his professional skills and tastes – with regard to Anglo Saxon, Middle English and alliterative poetry – were due to his West Midlands genes as much as anything else.[5] And he wrote to his son Christopher, informing him that he should regard his Tolkien inheritance as negligible: in truth he was Mercian or Hwiccian through and through.[6] It's worth noting, too, that the Anglo-Saxon texts of Lowdham's father in *The Notion Club Papers* are in ninth-century Mercian.

The first point to note about Tolkien's remark to Christopher on their ancestry is his willingness to disregard the Tolkien lineage, which was 200 years old and on the record, as it were – it was known that his father's family had migrated from Saxony – in favour of one that was entirely speculative and dated back a further 800 to 1,300 years. It was an emotional identification, not a rational one. It must have been based at least in part on a desire to bind himself more closely to his beloved, martyred mother and the brief spell of happiness they had shared in the Worcestershire countryside. But it must also have been motivated by a desire to find, even create, roots for himself in a culture for which he felt an extraordinary affinity, despite – or perhaps because of – its ultimate defeat.

There is also the literature of the area, most notably the works contained in a single document now in the British Library, part of the bequest to the nation of the manuscript collection belonging to the Elizabethan magnate and antiquarian Sir Robert Cotton. It contains the only known copies of *Sir Gawain and the Green Knight* and *Pearl*, which Tolkien edited and translated, together with two further religious poems, *Cleanness* and *Patience*. All four of these poems are usually regarded as being the work of a single unknown author writing in a northwest Midlands dialect, perhaps in Staffordshire, some time in the 14th century. They share a stylistic and structural complexity, and a command of the language, that places them on a par with the works of their presumed contemporary, Geoffrey Chaucer. Tolkien, given his preoccupation with loss, must have been pained by the circumstances of their transmission to us, its arbitrariness and dependence on luck. Cotton had built up an extraordinary and uniquely rich library of manuscripts, which also included the Lindisfarne Gospels and the only extant copy of *Beowulf*. He was one of the first people to consider such things worth collecting in the first place and certainly the only one to do it on such an extensive scale. However, many of them were destroyed in a fire on 23 October 1731; some were saved only by being thrown out of windows. The scale of the damage is hard to quantify. Initial estimates said that 212 of the 958 manuscript volumes were either entirely burned or seriously impaired. However, developments in conservation and restoration have rescued many of these, albeit not necessarily in their entirety. On the other hand, some volumes at first thought saved had nevertheless sustained substantial damage, among them the one containing *Beowulf*.

Even Cotton's magnificent collection is only part of the story. After all, there must have been innumerable manuscripts that did not survive even until the 16th century. In a pre-literate culture there must have been yet more poems and tales in circulation, like those about Wade at a later date, which were never even recorded and therefore died out of memory. It is a point that Tolkien would make in his landmark essay on *Beowulf,* 'The Monster and the Critics'. Readers would be mistaken to regard *Beowulf* as a primitive work, he said, to see it as standing at the beginning of a great literary tradition. It is rather a work created from the remnants of an ancient and no less great culture, which even then was fading, and which now is wholly lost.[7]

Professionally, Tolkien was an outsider. His academic career was littered with intra-departmental skirmishes over the proper extent of a university English degree. For many of his colleagues the periods and genres of literature in which he specialized were at best a tedious backwater and at worst an irrelevance. Woody Allen's joke – 'Just don't take any course where they make you read *Beowulf*' – probably articulates the position as well as anything. Yet Tolkien seems to have been temperamentally suited to the margins, to sifting through the rubble of a lost culture and aiding in its reconstruction. There's a good analogy for his overriding interest in rescuing the last remains of oral traditions from oblivion in the field of linguistic paleontology, which was in vogue in the late 19th century. Linguists had become increasingly interested in the points at which the seemingly irreconcilable family of Indo-European languages intersected, clearly revealing common roots. They thought that, with enough careful study, they would eventually be able to identify our earliest ancestors. As Colin Renfrew explains:

> By building up the vocabulary of Proto-Indo-European in this way – the protolexicon, as it has sometimes been called – it should be possible to construct some sort of picture of the world of these people and of their environment before their supposed dispersal from their hypothetical homeland, the *Urheimat*, as German scholars termed it.[8]

Tolkien felt keenly the absence of that kind of cultural homeland, or core body of folklore and myth, for the English. Whatever this might have contained it would always have been in antithesis to what most of us, heirs of the Renaissance as we are, regard as European culture, which looks south to the Mediterranean basin and the classical world for its inspiration. I suspect that that in itself made Mercia attractive to him: in one letter to his son Christopher he rails energetically against what he regards as an American-led cosmopolitanism, which he fears will reduce the world to a dull, suburban homogenous mass. He might well find a good many supporters for such a view, but it is unlikely that most would follow him in his wholly characteristic proposal for an act of defiance: an insistence on speaking exclusively Old Mercian.[9] Even in the context of English literature, the fact that the *Gawain* poet (as the unknown author mentioned above is usually known) was evidently not part of the metropolitan elite of Parliament or the king's court in London – unlike Chaucer or John Gower – and that therefore work of a very high quality could lie unread and forgotten for centuries in a single manuscript while Chaucer, say, made an early transition to print, made Tolkien that much fiercer in its defence. Any one act of cultural subjugation or marginalization could stand for all of them.

At the White Horse, the highest point in Oxfordshire, it is essentially Mercia that you look out on to the north. Standing there, I could see the storm I'd driven through away to the east, black clouds almost obliterating the eastern horizon, erasing the great cooling towers of the power station at Didcot. The north is gentler, an open plain made lovable by husbandry, with sugar-brown fields, their crops the colour of summer ale or broken cakes. Some fields, already harvested, were scattered with bales of hay, occasionally wrapped in powder-blue plastic sheets. There is a slight ridge in the middle distance that drew my eye: it's crowned with trees, against the grey of the far distant horizon. I was at the horse's head, contemplating the tradition that it is lucky to stand in its eye, something of which English Heritage understandably disapproves. Tolkien, I know, believed in luck as a kind of providential agent. Who would benefit from my setting foot on the white horse's eye and looking out over Mercia?

To the left of where I stood there is a bend in the road at the base of the hill holding a small bullet-shaped valley of trees; beyond there is a spire, and a village is gathered round it. This is, perhaps, what most people think of when they think of the countryside of southern England: hedged fields laid out across a gently rolling landscape as far as the eye can see, and trees erupting through the measured farmland as if welling up from the earth. There is a neatness or civility to it that you don't find elsewhere in the country, although it is, in fact, true only of a small area of England, running in an arc from the West Midlands down towards the Sussex Downs and the Weald of Kent.

Whatever we might like to think, the whole of this landscape has been shaped by human beings. In some ways the sound of the cars in the road below is no less authentic and natural than the horse itself, or the hill it lies on. The countryside here is not a recent invention either. We may react with horror to forest clearance in the Third World, but it is something that was wrought in England centuries, even millennia, ago. By the time the Romans arrived the greater part of the ancient primeval woodland had been taken for farming, mostly by the Celts. The first settlements were on hilltops, as here at the Iron Age hill-fort of Uffington Castle, which crowns White Horse Hill, a few minutes' walk back up past the horse itself, through thistle-thick long grass flecked with purple and orange wild flowers.

Although 'castle' might be thought to be an ambitious term for what is these days no more than earthworks, it is nevertheless still true that, even without the timber walls that stood on the banks, it is a commanding site, with authoritative views of all points on the compass from its periphery. The centre is a different story. If you wade through the tall grass into the concave circle, sunken and empty, all you can see is the sky above and a level, vertiginously flat field of grass that seems to rise up before you like a sea wall. It also doubles as a disturbingly foreshortened horizon. The world seems to stop at the far side of the circle, perhaps 50 feet away. Save for the absence of a standing stone, it reminded me strongly of the saucer-like hill-top where the hobbits sleep on the downs before falling prey to the barrow wights. We know nothing about the people who built it or those who may have lived here later. When it was excavated in the 19th century a single coin was found, belonging to the Dobunni, a Belgic tribe whose lands (as noted in Chapter 3) stretched from Lydney in the west to Wood Eaton on the east. They were relatively late arrivals to these islands, however, and are unlikely to have been responsible for this fort.

From such settlements people went out to clear the outlying forest and scrub, which then enabled them to move down into the valleys nearer the water supply of the rivers. In Anglo-Saxon times 'the essential familiar pattern of the English countryside – broad tracts of cultivated land and pasture punctuated with copses and limited stands of trees – had already been established'.[10] The trees and hedgerows that may seem immemorial to us are most likely no more than natural windbreaks planted by farmers to protect their exposed crops. It is now accepted that William the Conqueror bequeathed to his successor a country with no more than 15 per cent of its area under woodland, although this is, it should be said, a relatively recent conclusion. The consensus during Tolkien's lifetime was that 'the story of Anglo-Saxon settlement, when looked at in depth, yields more of the saga of man against forest than of Saxon against Celt'.[11]

To the west beyond the horse's head the hill falls away in strong supple folds, cradling a flat basin of land below, its floor smooth as sand beneath the tide. This is known now as the Manger, as it is supposedly where the horse feeds at night. It's where the cheese-rolling contests used to take place. The Saxons, however, knew it as the *hrung putt* or 'circle pit' (the first word being the root of the modern word 'ring'). We know this because we still have a large number of Anglo-Saxon boundary charters for the county, drawn up to define parishes and estates. They usually date from between 930 and 985, with the years between 940 and 960 being particularly well-represented. The names of two of them leap out: Buckland, to the northwest, and Bucklebury, to the south. Both of these still exist as villages. Unfortunately they are both also common English place names, deriving from the practice of 'booking' land to the church by charter. As Shippey notes, Tolkien was probably simply keen to create an etymology for them that tied them more closely to people and land, rather than contract law or the church. Even he found such derivations dull.[12]

There are other things of interest in the charters. I was struck, for instance, by the frequent use of the word *gara* – 'gore' in modern English – to describe the triangles of land left unploughed in asymmetrical fields. It's one of the archaic words that Haldir uses to describe the Naith of Lorien to Frodo and his companions. Another word that Haldir uses is 'Angle', recalling the historic home of the Angles, forefathers of the English and, more specifically, the Mercians, in northern Germany.[13] It's easy to focus on the Shire as the receptacle of all things English in *The Lord of the Rings*: easy, but mistaken. As here, and as with Rohan, there are subtle echoes throughout the novel, barely audible grace notes prefiguring the English settlement.

The charters also record, through their place names, the extent to which Tolkien's beloved northern mythology was integral to English life before the Norman Conquest, and the way the landscape was vivified by their presence. Wayland's Smithy itself offers a rare window of continuity through the millennia. To reach it from the White Horse you have to walk along the Ridgeway, the remains of a prehistoric track that once bisected southern England from the Dorset coast to the Wash. What we have now is some 85 miles long, running from Overton Hill, a mile or two from the great stone circle at Avebury in Wiltshire, up to Ivinghoe Beacon in Buckinghamshire, to the northeast of Aylesbury. The Ridgeway is much diminished in other ways too. Although the Romans seem to have avoided it – the first written reference to it dates from the Anglo-Saxon period – it was used by both travellers and farmers droving livestock until early modern times. As its name suggests, it holds to the crest of the hills, above both the spring line and the more difficult wooded terrain in the valleys. With the enclosure of land in the 17th and 18th centuries the Ridgeway became constricted: where there were once multiple paths to choose from, now it is hedged and fenced down to a single track.

Even given all this, you can't help but feel a sense of continuity, however tenuous that might be, when you walk along it. By Uffington the chalky subsoil makes the path white as bone, as if this was in fact the ancient spine of England. Not being a purist, I'm not too troubled by the fact that the growth of the banks and hedgerows where butterflies flit in the sunlight is a recent development: change is what gives survival meaning. It seems right, then, to look up from a Bronze Age path and see a passenger jet high in the stratosphere, twin vapour trails fading in the pale blue, softly clouded sky, the shout of its engines just in earshot in the still June heat. To the north poppies flourish brightly among the green crops of the ripening fields; it's a flower that could stand as an analogue for the Evermind or *simbelmynë* of Rohan.

The barrow of Wayland's Smithy is off the Ridgeway, to the right as you come from Uffington. It sits on a low, flat mound that tapers slightly to the north and is harboured by an imperfect ring of beech trees; the barrow itself must be in shadow almost the whole day. If you look at it head on, it's hard to escape metaphors of mouth and teeth. Its entrance is guarded by four spearhead-shaped sarsens, or sandstone boulders, which stand some eight or nine feet high, perhaps dragged from as far away as Marlborough. They are intimidating, but also seem oddly ill at ease with the neat dry-stone walling to either side of them, which is presumably more recent – as, one imagines, are the steps that lead onto the mound. These seemed particularly strange; I'm not used to being invited to walk on a grave, even when its inhabitants have been disinterred.

The mouth of the barrow is inviting, worryingly so, opening out into small, musty empty chambers, chilly even on a fine summer's day. Once you allow it its mouth and teeth, it's hard to keep from following the metaphor through into a vague pre-rational fear of being swallowed up by the cold earth as you look further into the dark corners of the tomb. I can't say I'd like to come at night, all things being equal. Those who do, judging from the scorched grass a few feet away, feel the need for fire, and perhaps not just for warmth or food. The two beech trees framing the mouth are covered in scratched or carved initials, almost all illegible, which, I guess, defeats the object of attaching yourself to history's margins. Out of arm's reach the swirls and whorls in the bark are like the current of a grey muddy stream. The boughs are fluent, graceful, like dancers; the leaves are lime-shaped and green like limes in the sunlight, with a hint of grey, like rosemary.

You can certainly project some sadness or sorrow onto the site, if you are of a mind to do so, perhaps particularly now that it has been stripped of its human cargo and therefore robbed of its primary function. Burial rituals, and the associated idea of memorializing the dead as an emotional or spiritual necessity, go back to the earliest periods in known human history, some 300,000 years ago. It has been argued that that in itself indicates a definitive stage in the development of human consciousness. Other animals are aware of death, but only human beings seek to mark the deaths of individuals in perpetuity, fixing them forever into the cycle of the seasons and the passing clouds of human habitation across the landscape. Arwen might be an exemplar of this, her green grave resting on Cerin Amroth until the end of time, part of the landscape long after she herself has been forgotten. In pre-literate societies, in particular, death and memory went hand in hand, since life could have no record but a burial site or a fistful of stories passed down from father to daughter, mother to son.

There is a good example of the ambivalence of all this a few miles to the southwest of Uffington, on the Lambourn Downs. Just outside Lambourn, to the north, is Seven Barrows Down, pitched on the low incline of a hill by a single track road. When we think of barrows on the downs in the context of Tolkien, the immediate reference is generally to the barrow wights and that sense of pervasive evil, of malignant spirits infusing the landscape with a cold and captivating dread. Yet the grave of Arwen and the burial mounds of the Rohirric kings outside Edoras are shadows with the same source, inverted earthen ships like these rising on the soft roll of northern fields. The irony of such grave-making is not lost on Tolkien. They are a claim on eternity against the depredations of time, a plea for remembrance. The tension is implicit in the exchange between Aragorn and Legolas about the five hundred years and 16 generations of men that the mounds of Rohan mark, which are as nothing to the elves. Yet elves and men such as these have been alike forgotten, have fallen out of memory: it is the central conceit of Middle Earth. Here on the Berkshire Downs, too, we know nothing of the people whose human care made the Lambourn barrows possible, still less the identities of the lost laid beneath them, their triumphs or their defeats.

You may half-expect some degree of spectral eeriness to infest any ancient burial site. I certainly did, the more so because I didn't reach Lambourn until dusk, when the moon was full and bright, but still close to the horizon, and the lights of the village were hidden around a curve in the road. The acrid bite of smoke drifted through the cooling air from a bonfire a little way back south. It is hard to articulate, but the *genius loci* here was anything but unworldly and dark; it was old, but, if anything, familiar and weary. For some reason, even over millennia this felt as much like a place for sorrow and reflection as any contemporary graveyard or cemetery, as much as Wolvercote, for instance (see Chapter 2). One of the things that had struck me about Wolvercote was the apparent move towards the use of photographs of the deceased set into headstones, something that I know has been common elsewhere in Europe for some while. If I had thought about it beforehand, I would probably have dismissed it as rather tasteless thing to do, as if such a judgement were an appropriate response to another's grief. Faced with it in fact – seeing traditional etched marble stones embedding blurred, casual photos of a moment's unthought-of happiness, young men and women remembered in all the beauty and foolishness of their youth – I found it unbearably moving. At Lambourn the poignancy derives from the opposite, the simple absence of identity, as if such barrows, like the various national monuments to unknown warriors, stood for the sorrows of all the vanished peoples of the Earth.

There is a kind of peace at Wayland's Smithy too. It is a lonely peace, perhaps, but a peace nonethless, amid the trees, their boughs reaching down, stretching, not quite reaching, to touch the tops of the stones. Yet because we know more about the site it is easier to see how conditional our understanding of it really is. Any such sentiments are self-evidently projections of our own emotions and beliefs. We know, for instance, that the site was built some time between 2300 and 1800 BC. While one's instinct may be to regard the landscape and any natural element within it as immemorial, it is risky to do so. The beech trees that surround the site and seem so integral to it today are essentially modern intrusions. Both beeches and firs were planted around the turn of the 19th century; even in the relatively short time since then the firs have disappeared. Obviously there is a point to be made about our transience and the survival of the mound, as if some notional kind of time-lapse photography could reveal the barrow as the still centre of a blurred whorl of human history. Yet as much as we may recognize the accuracy of this, we are nevertheless in that stream ourselves, believing as we rush on past that our momentary glimpse of this thing can define it absolutely.

Perhaps Wayland's Smithy also has darker undercurrents because of the stories that have become attached to it over the centuries. The best-known of the stories is very well-known indeed. It seems to have gone through something of a vogue in late Victorian and Edwardian England, since it crops up in Thomas Hughes's *Tom Brown's Schooldays*, Sir Walter Scott's *Kenilworth* and Rudyard Kipling's *Puck of Pook's Hill*. (The last of these is by far the best retelling.) In essence the story is, as recorded by Francis Wise in 1758:

> At this place lived formerly an invisible Smith; and if a traveller's horse had lost a shoe upon the road, he had no more to do, than to bring the horse to this place with a piece of money and leaving them both there for some little time, he might come again and find the money gone, but the horse new shod.

In itself this is a charming, if unremarkable piece of folklore. That Wise fails to name Wayland or connect him to his real ancestry should not concern us: as we will shortly see, there is no question as to the historicity of the site's name. The true – or at least more ancient – version of Wayland's story is rather more brutal and unpleasant.

Wayland was the son of Wade (see Chapter 4). He was apprenticed by his father to a race of elves renowned for their mastery of metalworking. Such was his skill, however, that he quickly outstripped them, to his misfortune: his reputation reached the ears of Niduth, the King of Sweden, who had him captured and enslaved. To ensure that Wayland could not escape and offer his craft to Niduth's enemies, Niduth had him hamstrung. Wayland bided his time until one day, when the king's two sons came to him requiring some work, he killed them both. Worse, he took their skulls and fashioned them into drinking vessels, watching as the king drank from them in ignorance. For good measure Wayland then raped the king's daughter, Baduhild or Beahhild, who had asked him to make her a ring, before escaping using a pair of wings that he had made for himself. Baduhild subsequently bore him a son called Wittick.

The relevance of this tale is revealed in the history of the landscape. Wayland's Smithy itself crops up in a boundary charter for Compton Beauchamp dated AD 955. Leslie Grinsell, researching the area in the 1930s for his book *White Horse Hill and the Surrounding Country*, probably at much the same time as Tolkien was entertaining his children, also notes of this charter that:

> It mentions a mound, called *hwittic's hlaew* (Hwittic's mound) which may be identified…with a natural knoll east of Compton Beauchamp and just north of Hardwell Wood and the Icknield Way, just over a mile north of Wayland's Smithy.

Moreover, another charter, for Woolstone, mentions *beahhilds byrigels* – 'Beahhild's burial place' – some two miles to the northwest. It's possible that there were further concordances. In a recent article in the magazine *Archaeology* David Hinton suggests – tentatively, it has to be said – that the Anglo-Saxon boundary mark of *eceles beorh* could mean 'Ecel's barrow', recalling the name of

Egil, one of Wayland's brothers.[14]

While it is only fair to note that some of Grinsell's scholarship hasn't gone unchallenged, his research was certainly accepted while Tolkien was active. Tolkien, I think, would have looked at this and thought about the way in which myth and landscape become intertwined, the meanings of one being used to vivify the experience of the other; or, to put it another way, how a people understood their homelands through – sometimes literally – the actions of myth upon it. He would no doubt also have reflected that a mythic sense of place such as this had been allowed to drain from the culture as much as from the landscape, and that where there were once many such stories entrenched in the rivers, hills and fields of England, most had now gone. Even here only Wayland's Smithy itself was remembered and the myth itself had been worn down into an anodyne ghost of its former self, the vengeful smith now faded to invisibility, working for mere pence on a hill on the Mercian border.

It's arguable that Wayland has survived at all only because he was already a major figure, appearing in many places throughout early Germanic and Scandinavian literature, most notably in *Volund's Saga*. But he has a presence in Anglo-Saxon verse as well: for instance, it is Wayland who forges Beowulf's armour. He also finds his way into the Exeter Book, a priceless collection of Old English literature that includes *The Seafarer*, *The Wayfarer* and *Crist*. Alongside these the book preserves a 42-line poem known as *Déor*. It records the lament of Déor, a minstrel, who has been supplanted in his king's affections by a rival named Heorrenda. Déor enumerates the suffering of great figures down the ages, among them

Weyland in Niduth's prison, and hopes that, like theirs, his suffering will in time pass.

If we didn't feel sure that Tolkien knew all this professionally, we can see him using it in *The Book of Lost Tales*. In one version Aelfwine of England is described as Déor's son, while Eriol fathers Heorrenda in Tol Eressëa, for better or worse by a mother different from Hengist and Horsa's. Another version tells us that the Book of Lost Tales itself is going to be compiled by Heorrenda of Haegwudu from his father's notes. 'Haegwudu' is Old English for Great Haywood, which (as mentioned above) is about 20 miles from Offa of Mercia's capital at Tamworth. However, any readers unfamiliar with Tolkien's unpublished writings, as reproduced in Christopher Tolkien's 12-volume *History of Middle Earth*, should be aware that there are often numerous versions or sketches of different stories, which frequently contradict one another. I've simply tried to suggest connections in this book to illustrate the way in which Tolkien responded to both English landscapes and the idea of England. One result of this approach is that differences, subtle or otherwise, among the many strands of his work will necessarily be blurred, if not obliterated.

The loss of Beahhild from the English landscape could simply reflect a process of cultural change, as new myths erase the old. Hence, as the Germanic culture of the Angles and the Saxons declined in the second millennium, so the people living on the downs sought new metaphors for their identity. *Eceles beorh* is still to be found a little way from Wayland's Smithy. Indeed, it lies below the tail of the White Horse. It is known as Dragon Hill and the myths that supplanted the rich complexity of the northern

European culture of the first millennium were narrow, nationalist ones. As you might guess from its name, the myth in question here is that of St George and the Dragon.

From the perspective of the White Horse, Dragon Hill down below seems almost an afterthought and barely, in fact, a hill. It is a large flat-topped, steep-sided mound. Before I saw it I had read that its peak had been flattened and, having been to sites in Mexico such as Monte Alban, I was expecting something with a little drama or flair to it. Disappointingly, it looks as if the levelling Dragon Hill was the work of a weekend. However, towards its further edge is a bare patch of chalk shaped like a hunting horn or a crescent opening. The story is that it was here that St George slew the dragon and that where its blood fell the grass no longer grows, hence the chalky rock beneath breaking through. Among other things this has the benefit of convenience, since it also explains the white horse as belonging to St George, although some would still contend that the horse is not a horse at all but a representation of a dragon. The absence of wings is not apparently regarded as a problem with this theory.

In any event, we can see another transition in the folklore of the area sandwiched between Wayland and St George. Francis Grose, writing in *The Antiquities of England and Wales* towards the end of the 18th century, noted that:

> Uffington Castle, near White Horse Hill, is supposed to be Danish, and near it is Dragon Hill, supposed to be the burying place of Uter Pendragon, a British prince. Near White Horse Hill are the remains of a funeral monument of a Danish chief slain at Ashdown by Alfred.

Here we have echoes of a different nationalist myth, that of the native resistance to the attacks of the Danes, which did more than most to destroy the diversity of the English nation. But in Uter Pendragon we also have a link to the myth, which post-dates the Norman Conquest, of Arthur and his defence of Celtic Britain from the Saxons. Grose may well have known that not far from Uffington, to the southwest, lies the village of Liddington, which many claim is the site of Arthur's last, victorious battle at Mount Badon, usually dated to the early 500s.

Having inspected Dragon Hill, I climbed the path back to the White Horse. In the folds of the hill to my right, above the Manger, the grasses seemed to lie in strata, alert and erect despite the full wind, as if somehow being combed against the grain. I looked back out across the counties of the Mark. It is a major feat of will to see all this as Tolkien imagined it, to strip away the civility of this landscape, the generations of care and tenderness, the hedgerows, the neat villages, the spires, the black roads, to strip it all back to when it was truly wild, still, perhaps, forested, or at the moment when human beings first began to fashion it to their needs, when they could have stood in the shallow basin at the top of the hill, gazing out into the unknowable distance and wondering what the warm wind from the north foretold, what the eastern storm foreboded.

Chapter Nine
Rollright, Oxfordshire/Warwickshire

It would be a mistake to assume that Tolkien's conception of the South Downs to the east of the Old Forest is limited to sources on the Berkshire Downs, central though they are to it. Almost as important as the barrows are the standing stones, which Tolkien imported to the downs from Rollright further north, on the border between Warwickshire and Oxfordshire. (Rollright also appears in *Farmer Giles of Ham*, though it is not mentioned by name: Tolkien said in a letter that Rollright is where the dog meets the dragon in that story.)[1]

The Rollright stones are roughly equidistant between Stratford upon Avon and Oxford, to the north and south, and Banbury and Stow-on-the-Wold, to the east and west. They were a little hard to find, however, since, for some reason, they didn't appear on any road signs until I was about a mile away. I had to head for Little Rollright and hope for the best. It was autumn by the time I made it there. The air was cold and wet, and, appropriately enough, a thick mist was ebbing and flowing around the site.

There are three sets of stones at Rollright: the King's Stone; the

Whispering Knights, also known as the Five Knights; and a stone circle known as the King's Men. Despite appearances they date from radically different periods and stand in separate fields. These fields are divided by a narrow, high-hedged road that presumably marks the boundary between Oxfordshire and Warwickshire: as we shall see, two of the sets of stones are in the former county, one is in the latter.

The meaning of the name 'Rollright' can only be conjectured. It is probably Anglo-Saxon in origin, meaning something like 'Rolla's landright'; the name 'Hrolla' has been found in a Saxon land charter relating to Rollington by Wilton, near Salisbury. There is, however, a contrary theory, noted by Grinsell, which suggests that the name derives from the Frankish heroic romance *Le chanson de Roland* (*The Song of Roland*), which was once so well-known that, it is said, it was sung by the Norman soldiers at the Battle of Hastings to keep up their morale. This would place the origin of the name early in the second millennium. In any event the name is certainly applied to an area larger than just the vicinity of the stones. Aside from Little Rollright there is Great Rollright a couple of miles to the east. The names are a little misleading, however: Great Rollright is a tiny village, while Little Rollright is so small that it doesn't even appear on my road map and I never found it at all. The whole area is rich in remains: archaeologists have found Bronze Age barrows and Iron Age settlements; a Roman settlement from the mid-period of the colonization; and an early Saxon cemetery dating from around 600.

The King Stone is the only one located in Warwickshire. It's a sarsen, a standing stone, some seven or eight feet high, sticking up out of the soil like a bone or a clenched fist. It's sited a little short of the top of a low hill that was once thought to be a barrow. Sadly it's now railed off so you can't get close to it. Just beyond the railings, to the north, there is what I took to be an elder, which was quite bare at the time of year I saw it, apart from a few clusters of drying berries. Around the field the leafless trees were thick with ivy, although to the south the deceptive pitch of the ridge is sufficient to obscure the land beyond, a fact that has found its way into the rich folklore of the area.

The King Stone marks a Bronze Age cemetery dating from between 1800 and 1500 BC, but that has been long forgotten. The myths about the King Stone – and the Rollright stones in general – centre on petrification, the turning of human beings to stone through the agency of witchcraft. Specifically, the core of the tale is that the stones collectively represent a king, his knights and his army. The king aspired to conquer England. It is said that he was challenged by a witch to take seven strides forward. If he could see Long Compton in the valley below him his wish to rule the country would be granted. On his seventh stride, however, the land rose up in front of him, blocking his view. The witch then said:

> As Long Compton thou canst not see
> King of England thou shalt not be.
> Rise up stick and stand still stone
> For King of England thou shalt be none;
> Thou and thy men hoar stones shall be
> And I myself an eldern tree.

It's a little difficult to tell with the railings in place, but I made it six paces from the King's Stone before I could see Long Compton, which I could do quite easily despite the mist, perhaps because it lies in the valley below the hill, where the air was clearer. If he was a king, therefore, he was clearly no judge of distance. But perhaps the story simply exists to explain the way the land miraculously appears beneath you as you take the last step.

This is certainly an old story, but it is hard to know which elements of it are original and which are later additions. When it and the stones first appear in the record, in Camden's *Britannia*, it feels like only a partial account, but it may reflect simply an earlier stage in its development:

> The highest of [the Rollright Stones] they use to call the King, because he should have been the King of England if had once seen Long Compton, a little town lying beneath, and which a man, if he go some five paces forward, may see.

Perhaps the witch didn't figure when the tale was first told. It is certainly tempting to date her role to the 17th century or later, given the general indifference to witchcraft before that time, but there's no evidence on which to do so. Yet Camden appears to be offering a partial account, since it is hard to see by what agency the king was petrified.

It is, however, interesting to note the subtext of native resistance to foreign incursion and subjugation, which is also present in some of the myths surrounding the White Horse and Dragon Hill. On this reading the witch stands for a popular culture and system of beliefs threatened by the army of the King. In any event, the theme is made more explicit in a version of the tale from 1705 unearthed by Leslie Grinsell, which specifically locates it towards the end of the first millennium. It runs:

> Said the Danish General
> If Long Compton I could see
> The King of England I should be.
> But replied the Saxon General
> Then rise up hill and stand fast stone
> For King of England thou'lt be none.

The Danes first attacked England in 835, when they raided the Isle of Sheppey off the coast of Kent. The succeeding decades found the English, more or less united under Alfred the Great of Wessex and then his son Edward, alternately fighting and treating with the Viking invaders. The Danes used the great estuaries of the Thames, the Severn and the Humber to reach deep into the country, with devastating effects.

It's a period that Tolkien planned to draw on in his unfinished work, *The Lost Road*. One section was to feature Aelfwine of England, born in the year the Danes first appeared on our shores, living at the court of King Edward some 80 years later, around 914 or 915. The raiders have attacked (as they did in reality) Porlock and Watchet on the North Somerset coast. Aelfwine and some friends escape by sea and, after being harried by the Vikings near Lundy, an island in the Severn estuary, find themselves on the lost straight road.

There are other kinds of folklore attached to the King Stone.

One is the custom of gathering at the stones on Midsummer Eve and finding the elder tree in blossom. The tree would be cut and, as it bled, the King Stone would slowly move its head. Perhaps inevitably, there are also stories of fairies, who, it was said, used to rise up out of a hole in the ground near the stone and dance around it at night. If ever children tried to block the hole with rocks or stones, it would be mysteriously cleared by the next morning. If I had found it I'd have blocked it myself. I feel that I would have had Tolkien's blessing in doing so: he detested the tweeness of this kind of thing, not least, perhaps, because he himself had indulged in it as a young man, most notably in a poem called 'Goblin Feet', dating from April 1915 and reproduced in part in Carpenter's biography. Towards the end of his life he told an interviewer from the *Sunday Times*:

> I don't like small creatures. If there was anything that I detested it was all of that Drayton stuff; hideous. All that hiding in cowslips.[2]

Across the road and a little further along are the Whispering Knights, the oldest of the three sites at Rollright. This group was in origin a burial chamber dating from between 3800 and 3000 BC. One of its five stones has fallen: it previously rested on the other four, which are still upright. The whole group originally sat beneath a long cairn. The knights too are circled with iron railings. They looked particularly forlorn on the day I saw them, being enclosed in a wider circle of mist and positioned towards the edge of an outsized modern field, which was regular, green and even with next year's crop. So broad is the field that even on a clear day, I imagine, its furthest edge would be lost over the gentle camber of the land. It's easy to see where their name came from, since they are huddled close together: when I saw them it seemed to be for shelter, but on other days it may seem more conspiratorial. The stones are deeply pitted: the holes worn in them by wind and rain over the centuries push far beneath the surface, as if they were fingermarks pressed into sand. One stone is almost worn through in places. It is easy enough, if you wish to, to see bleak faces staring blankly back at you out of prehistory, like the Púkel men of Dunharrow. Behind them the thick hedge that runs the length of the field opens up, making them seem yet more vulnerable and exposed.

From the Whispering Knights I could see the King's Men, tucked privately away in the northwestern corner of the field, a small enclave protected on three sides by trees, open only to the south. I couldn't reach them across the field, however. This being active farmland, I had to go back to the road and walk along.

Built some time between 2500 and 2000 BC, the King's Men form the easternmost extant stone circle in Britain. It is about 100 feet across. When the stones were first laid out there were some 103 of them, forming a closed circle with one entrance only. Now there are far fewer. The Rollright Trust says that there are 77, although I could only count 73: in my defence I should mention that it isn't always obvious where one stone begins and another ends. Counting them seemed a necessary thing to do, since there is a myth that it is impossible. If I was hoping to be bewitched I was disappointed, although it did score high on the scale of dull things to do in the country. Whoever first described them as resembling teeth was on the money: they look like the rotted stumps of teeth, carious and uneven. Close up they aren't uniform in colour either, being patchworks of black, white, grey, dun, torp and beige, overlaid with islands of lichen the colour of English mustard, some of which themselves date back 800 years.

Through the opening to the south the mist had closed down the horizon to half a field away, where an oak loomed out of the hedgerow. Over to the left the Whispering Knights were no more than a vague shadow, lost from this perspective against the dark mass of the hedge behind. For some reason most of the stories attached to the stones centre on the theme of impossibility. I have mentioned counting them, but there are other tales of what has befallen those who have tried to move them against their 'will'. Grinsell relates one about the tallest stone among the King's Men, which was moved to mend a bridge over the stream at Little Rollright. Two men were killed on the journey down, which also required four horses, so heavy was the stone. After the men were buried in the churchyard at Little Rollright the stone was returned to its rightful place: this time only a single horse was needed. Another story tells how a miller took the same stone to dam his mill pond, but however much water was collected during the day it would drain away to nothing overnight.

It is all quite low-key, but the general thrust of this place is a kind of malevolence, content to stay within its own circle if unmolested, but vengeful if disturbed. All these stones seem to have a kind of autonomy. They do not belong to our world – and to that degree their being fenced off is wholly appropriate – but tolerate our co-existence. Other stories tell of the stones moving, going down to a nearby spring to drink at midnight on New Year's Eve. Like the stones that Frodo sees on the Barrow Downs in the fog, which have vanished in the clear light of day, their will is not ours to know. Petrified as they are, they are no longer human, but perhaps they still remember their humanity and over the long cold centuries have learned to hate those who still retain it.

Writing in 1895, A.J. Evans noted the myth that some day:

> the stones will turn into flesh and blood once more, and the King will stand as an armed warrior at the head of his army to overcome his enemies and make over all the land.

There is said to be a cave beneath the stones where the rest of the King's army waits for him. The return of the King, indeed – but it's a common enough trope, present in Arthurian legend but also attached to national heroes such as Sir Francis Drake. Here it is slightly more complex, given that it isn't entirely clear whether the King is on 'our' side or not, and it's a complexity that is carried over into *The Lord of the Rings*, I think, where it finds an echo in the Paths of the Dead that Aragorn takes from Dunharrow and the army that he gathers there.

By the time I left Rollright the sky was clearing to the south and a bright swathe of light rode above the dark, almost mauve cloud beneath. It was still cold and wet. There are things here that Tolkien would undoubtedly have loathed. On the way out I passed a sign advertising a conference, I think, to be held by an organization called the Pagan Federation. Among the speakers was a self-styled American pagan priestess; subjects covered include shamanism and the prehistoric use of drug plants.

It is possible that Tolkien liked the *idea* of the remote and ancient past rather than the thing itself. In *The Lost Road* Alboin's father tells him that the great age of Northern culture is lost forever, save for that small measure which has been accommodated by Christianity.[3]

I suspect that this was a situation that Tolkien was generally quite happy with. He was certainly ambivalent about paganism. You can see that doubleness in his use of the raw materials he found on the Downs and at such places as Rollright, turning stones and barrows alike into places of evil, as on the Barrow Downs, and sites of loss and sorrow and regret, as with the mounds of the men of Rohan, or the lost history of the makers of the Púkel men.

Chapter Ten
Fonthill, Wiltshire

In *The Treason of Isengard* Christopher Tolkien notes in passing that in its original form Wellinghall, the house of Treebeard in Fangorn, was named Fonthill, derived from the place of that name in Wiltshire. He knew this not least because his father havered between 'Fonthill' and 'Funtial', the name by which the site was known in an Anglo-Saxon charter. It means something like 'spring hill'.[1]

This did more than intrigue me. In the days when I read Tolkien incessantly the Ents were among my favourite elements. A tree woken from sleep or otherwise imbued with sentience is, of course, a common trope, recognizable in everything from the dryads of classical myth to the trees that pelt the Scarecrow with apples in *The Wizard of Oz*. But the way Tolkien developed that obviousness into the doomed Ents, forlorn shepherds of the trees – something much more complex and unusual – made such references irrelevant. As a child, perhaps, the fascination is with their otherness. Whereas talking animals in fables or fantasy are evidently human in their characters and concerns – offering the chance to feel a surrogate kinship with them – the Ents' perspective is alien, the embodiment by way of contrast of a theme apparent elsewhere in the book: the short, transient span of human life. It's not a sentiment that I can recall coming across much in anything else I read back then, even in books where characters died. As I grew older other themes emerged: in some ways, they are there to mark the passing of the primeval European forest; in others to reflect how humanity has flooded the rest of creation, drowned some and overrun the rest. Their behaviour under pressure offers a template from Tolkien's moral code. Ents, as we meet them in *The Lord of the Rings*, having lost their Entwives, can foresee that they are almost certain to die in oblivion; they have already dwindled into misshapen folk memory. Yet they have no power to change their destiny and only the merest vestiges of hope. Defeated as they are they still choose defiance, in accordance with the northern idea of courage that Tolkien admired so much in *Beowulf* and elsewhere.[2]

Above all, however, and most simply, the Ents articulate and embody Tolkien's own profound love for trees and wooded landscapes, both for what they are in themselves – objects of beauty and reverence – and for the link with the past that they represent through their longevity and persistence. I loved the Ents prodigiously, their slowness, their physical power, their essential loneliness.

Fonthill, then, seemed of more than passing interest. Wiltshire, however, is not a county I know well at all. I bought a map and found, to my surprise, that many of the place names down here seemed very Tolkienish – with regard to the Shire at least – at least as much as in his beloved Mercia. A cursory glance revealed, for example, Long Bottom, Coombe and Underhill. English place names have an absurd beauty of their own and have become a rich source of humour that other have mined more thoroughly, and with more wit, than I would ever be likely to. Yet casting around a couple of pages of my map-book revealed any number of villages and landmarks that I would like to have seen in the Shire, among them The Marshes, Scrubbed Oak, Snail-creep Hanging, The Middles and Cold Kitchen Hill. Puckwell Coppice recalls, at least to my mind, the Púkel men (discussed in Chapters 3 and 9). In a way this is less to say that Tolkien derived one from the other, but that their derivation from a common root makes the possibility of the latter – the core conceit of the book being that it is genuine folk history – seem more plausible.

I have no doubt that there are plenty more examples to be found by anyone who looked more thoroughly, but I am not sure how far that would get us. Tolkien was quite capable of liking names, their sounds, the way they roll around the tongue, irrespective of the hills and valleys they were moored to. Moreover, the way he constructed names was, essentially, based on that of the English record, so it is hardly surprising that there should be some overlap. On the other hand, unconscious echoes and borrowings can sometimes reveal significant things, whatever the author himself may or may not have thought about the results.

Anyway, it wasn't until late in the year, after the autumnal equinox, that a trip became possible. Fonthill isn't actually a long way from London, perhaps 130 miles or so, and some 30-odd miles southeast of Bath. Stonehenge is around 20 miles to the east. I suspect that, like me, many people know the county as somewhere that people pass through on their way to the 'real West Country', further down the A303. Off the motorway the roads become crowded with lorries that straddle the carriageway, and seem to bully their way through the small towns and villages.

Outside Westbury there is another white horse carved into the chalk hillside. This too was reputedly originally cut to commemorate one of Alfred's victories over the Danes, although the horse that can be seen today actually dates from the 18th century. While it undoubted looks more like an actual horse, it has none of the grace or energy of the one at Uffington (see Chapter 8). The horse here is standing still; it is like a child's figurine, inert and lifeless.

It was a fine day, with the sun low in the sky but bright, throwing long shadows across the dun fields even at noon. Most of the farmland I could see seemed to be pasture, sheep carelessly grazing the wet grass, but this didn't feel like a county grown fat on rich yielding soil. There's an austerity, almost a hardness, to it, which sharpens the senses, making the outbursts of woodland and the smooth low arcs of the hills peculiarly graceful. I thought of what Tolkien once told an interviewer about the Shire:

> It provides a fairly good living with moderate husbandry and is tucked away from all centres of disturbance; it comes to be regarded as divinely protected, though people there didn't realize it at the time. That's rather how England used to be, isn't it?[3]

Autumn is cold and its lights, as much as its mists, are always a source of pleasure. Slowly passing the turned fields by the roadside, I saw acres of white stubble like frost in the middle distance. The sense of the old year winding down, greenness gone into hiding, was powerful, an emotional presence clear as the thin chill air. Mist hung over the landscape well into the afternoon. Towards the horizon there was nothing but the ghosts of green fields, forests and wolds. All colour was drained from the land.

There are actually two villages at Fonthill – Fonthill Bishop and Fonthill Gifford – although the latter is really little more than a hamlet. It has a pub, the Beckford Arms, at the foot of the hill, but not even a shop that I could see. What I know of the area's history is of little relevance. The two villages reflect a division of ownership stretching back to the Norman Conquest. Fonthill Bishop belonged to the bishops of Winchester, under an Anglo-Saxon charter; Fonthill Gifford got its name from a grant of land by William the Conqueror to one Berengar Gifford, who had fought alongside him at the Battle of Hastings. If the area is known for anything, however (and that appears to be an optimistic opening), it is for William Beckford and Fonthill Abbey.

Born in 1760, Beckford was the richest man in Britain, thanks in part to the sugar plantations that his family owned in the West Indies. After a homosexual scandal forced him out of the country for a while, he returned to closet himself in the privacy of his family estate at Fonthill. Unhappy with the house that his father had had built, he became determined to commission a magnificent new property on a hill overlooking his 500-acre estate. It was to be modelled on the medieval cathedrals and given the name Fonthill Abbey. Built it was, on an extraordinary scale. Its central octagonal tower, for instance, was almost 300 feet high. Its doors were 35 feet high: there is a story that Beckford employed a dwarf to open them in order to magnify the sense of scale. Unfortunately, the cathedrals that Beckford wished to emulate had taken decades, sometimes centuries, to build and he wanted something quicker. The result was a building that looked magnificent but had major structural flaws. It survived less than 30 years and yet in that time the main tower collapsed six times.

A major part of Fonthill's story it may be, but it is hard to connect in any way to Tolkien. I hoped, even so, that a connection would become apparent on the hill itself, which rises up to the southwest of Fonthill Gifford. There are several approaches you can take. I tried those from Hindon and Fonthill Bishop. The former takes you south out of the village and quickly up into spacious woodland on the hillside, most of its greenness now fallen and lost. However, there are some fir trees and pines in among the oaks and ashes, and some plane trees too. The woods were the colour of tobacco and smoke the day I saw them, ferns spilling like gold out of the undergrowth and over the blackened, half-broken wall by the roadside. I hoped that one of the two roads on the map would take me to the hill's summit. I could see that one led to Bitham Lake, while the other, named the Great Western Avenue, had once led to the abbey and no doubt still led to its remains. Both, however, were closed and guarded by late Victorian or Edwardian lodges tucked into the sides of the drives, red-bricked and deep gabled where most other buildings are built of the grey local stone.

The day was getting on now and the pallid autumn light was beginning to thicken into dusk. I tried the Fonthill Bishop route, which took me through the original gateway to the estate and down a long straight road towards the hill. As at other great country houses, such as Blenheim Palace or, for that matter, Stonyhurst, the idea is that the visitor's eye is drawn by the line of the drive to the building around which the perspective is constructed. It is a statement of wealth and power, of ownership and status. Without Beckford's monumental home to make sense of the frame, the picture here seems distorted, disorienting, almost a trick. The road leads nowhere. The gate itself, adorned with stone urns but otherwise quite plain, now looks an extraordinary outsized thing, wholly dominating its surroundings. Two substantial walls line the approach to the gate, hemming in some woodland, but breaking off abruptly. It is as if someone had acquired Marble Arch and decided that it would make the greatest impact squashed into a small Wiltshire village.

I went down the drive, an ornamental lake to the left reflecting the falling leaves and bare trees of the adjacent wood. At the end I turned right, past the pub, and then up and round the corner of the hill onto the charmingly named Stop Street, itself a dead end. I parked my car and walked the path up onto the hillside. The wind was picking up; the rumour of it hissed in the tall trees. Through to the right ran a low wall, held together now only by the tight grip of the roots burrowed through it. Here, at least, on the eastern side of the hill there was still some vivid green on the forest floor, bright as lime.

My heart sank. I could see a small sign hung across the path ahead. I knew what it would say and I could already tell, from the disregard for potential readers evident in the way that it was placed, that it wasn't going to be a welcome. I read it in any case: 'Private. No Entry.' It felt like a defeat, a barring of the way into the last piece of Tolkien's England I'd set out to see.

Yet, looking back over the year, I felt that I had come close to an understanding of what Tolkien set out to achieve, and closer, too, to the man and his obsessions. More than that, I had begun to see England as I think he must have seen it: as a temperate and benign landscape reclaimed from the wild, written over, erased and rewritten by an endless succession of peoples, stretching back into the dark oblivion of antiquity. It is too much to hope to hear the voice of such peoples now, but we can still identify their marks on the fields and forests, in the place names that we may barely glance at as we drive past, still less considering their meanings and what that might tell us about our history.

I can see more clearly that *The Lord of the Rings* is in itself an act of rescue for an England vanished from the record, woven together from almost random glimpses of the past, odd snatched phrases or broken monuments. Yet it is too a valediction, an acknowledge-ment that change and loss are inexorable, and that all victories are tempered by the bitter undertow of defeat. I hazard the guess that Tolkien probably defined his England by the things lost from it, but also loved the tenacity of what survived, in folklore and myth, in language, in the very shapes of the hills and valleys.

Perhaps this journey to Fonthill had simply been meaningless, a futile chase after an elusive, unknowable quarry, based on nothing but a throwaway remark in a book of his notes, drafts and sketches. Perhaps for Tolkien the attraction of Fonthill had not been the place at all, but rather the breathy sound of the name, or the way the two elements were yoked together in a pleasing, euphonious marriage. Or perhaps it was simply the image they conjured up. After all, he retained it when he reinvented Fonthill as Wellinghall. I felt a little as he must have done when he came across the name 'Earendel', or the word 'woses', or the phrase '*orthanc enta geweorc*', in Anglo-Saxon poems (as mentioned in Chapter 7),[4] and strained after their meaning, trying to conceive of a context that would make sense of them and offset their awkwardness.

The things I wanted explained were the things that he mined from his own experience and learning, his own complex love of England, and his taste for language and myth. For all its openness his world is still the private world of a private man. No one will enter it fully again. Yet the journey to Fonthill still seemed valuable in itself, a small attempt to retrieve meaning, as Tolkien might have done, from the smallest of hints, and to understand just a little more of the England he adored.

I walked back to the car, watching the slow clouds in the sky and the boughs of the trees on the edge of the wood weaving unsteadily in the wind. A willow leant indifferently over a small pastured tract. A copse to the east seemed to be exploding like a cloud of dust and earth, grey dust and brown earth, out of the fields. The pale moon, not quite full, its brightness veiled still by the diminishing daylight, was already low in the sky as the sun sank into shadow on the far side of the hill.

Acknowledgements

First and foremost I would like to thank Sarah Such, without whom this book would not exist, and whose advice and encouragement have been unfailing. I am wholly in her debt.

I am also extremely grateful to Jonathan Hewat of Stonyhurst College and Sylvia Jones of Lydney Park, both of whom were very generous with their time and very patient with my questions.

Maggie Burns of Birmingham Library Services, Professor David Hinton of Southampton University, Joyce Millington of the Mercian Movement and Kevan White of roman-britain.org were all kind enough to provide me with information themselves or to point me in the right direction.

I would also like to thank Vivienne Mager, Alasdair Moore, Chris Riding and Vivienne Wilson for their friendship and support.

Above all, I would like to thank Helen, Isaac and Evie, both for making this book possible in the first place, and for tolerating elves and hobbits in the house for far longer than could ever be thought desirable. I could not have undertaken this without their love and this book is in every way dedicated to them.

Chapter Notes

All the sources mentioned are by J.R.R. Tolkien except as shown otherwise. Further details on each item can be found in the Bibliography.

Introduction
1 See in particular his 1951 letter to Milton Waldman in *Letters*, p. 144.
2 Review of A. Mawer and F.M. Stenton (eds), *Introduction to the Survey of English Place Names*, Vol. 1 (Cambridge University Press, 1924), under the heading 'Philology, General Works' in *The Year's Work in English Studies* (1924), p. 65.
3 For Christopher Tolkien's comment on this see *The Shaping of Middle Earth*, p. 174.
4 *The Book of Lost Tales*, Book I, p. 108.

Chapter 1 – A personal journey
1 In full: Jim Allan, *An Introduction to Elvish and to Other Tongues and Proper Names and Writing Systems of the Third Age of the Western Lands of Middle-Earth as Set Forth in the Published Writings of Professor John Ronald Reuel Tolkien.*
2 Interview with William Cater, *Sunday Times*, 2 February 1972.
3 Translation of the Durham Proverbs, no. 14, in Shippey, *The Road to Middle Earth*, p. 125.

Chapter 2 – Beginnings and endings

1 *Letters*, p. 221.

2 *The Book of Lost Tales*, Book II, p. 3.

3 Shippey, *The Road To Middle Earth*, p. 277.

4 Appendix F of *The Lord of the Rings*; and see the discussion of Froda and his Scandinavian analogue, Frothi, in Shippey, *The Road to Middle Earth*, pp. 185–8.

5 Interview with Philip Norman, *Sunday Times Magazine*, 15 January 1967.

6 Carpenter, *J.R.R. Tolkien: A Biography*, p. 106.

7 *Letters*, p. 9.

8 Carpenter, *J.R.R. Tolkien: A Biography*, p. 105.

Chapter 3 – The temple of Nodens at Lydney Park, Gloucestershire

1 R.E.M. Wheeler and T.V. Wheeler, *Report on the Excavation of the Prehistoric, Roman and Post-Roman Site in Lydney Park, Gloucestershire* (1932).

2 *Letters*, p. 333.

3 See the chapter 'The Muster of Rohan' in *The Lord of the Rings*.

4 See, for instance, *Letters*, p. 110.

5 Interview, *Paris Review*, Spring 2003.

6 *Archaeology*, issue 65, June 2002.

7 Wheeler and Wheeler (see note 1), p. 29.

8 *Letters*, p. 306.

9 *Letters*, p. 376.

Chapter 4 – The Lizard Peninsula, Cornwall

1 Shippey, *The Road to Middle Earth*, pp. 218–9.

2 *Sauron Defeated*, pp. 236–7.

3 *Letters*, p. 46.

4 Interview with Keith Brace, *Birmingham Post*, 23 May 1968.

5 *Letters*, pp. 78, 85.

6 'On Fairy Stories', in *The Monster and the Critics, and Other Essays*, p. 135.

7 *The Lost Road and Other Writings*, pp. 38–9.

8 Both quotations are from 'Philology, General Works', in *The Year's Work in English Studies* (1924).

9 Carpenter, *J.R.R. Tolkien: A Biography*, p. 98.

10 *Letters*, p. 213.

11 *The Lost Road*, p. 45.

12 See Appendix F of *The Lord of the Rings*; and Shippey, *J.R.R. Tolkien: Author of the Century*, p. 65.

13 *Sauron Defeated*, p. 119.

Chapter 5 – Oxford, Sarehole, Moseley, Birmingham

1 Shippey, *J.R.R. Tolkien: Author of the Century*, p. 63.

2 Interview, *Scotsman*, 25 March 1967; interview, *Oxford Mail*, 3 August 1966.

3 Shippey, *J.R.R. Tolkien: Author of the Century*, pp. 5–6.

4 *Letters*, p. 230; interview with Keith Brace, *Birmingham Post*, 23 May 1968.

5 Carpenter, *J.R.R. Tolkien: A Biography*, p. 24.

6 *Letters*, pp. 353–4.

7 Ibid., p. 416.

8 Ibid., p. 250.

9 Interview with Philip Norman, *Sunday Times Magazine*, 15 January 1967.

10 Interview with Keith Brace, *Birmingham Post*, 23 May 1968

11 Carpenter, *J.R.R. Tolkien: A Biography*, p. 129.

12 *The Treason of Isengard*, p. 216.

13 Carpenter, *J.R.R. Tolkien: A Biography*, p. 28.

14 Carpenter, *J.R.R. Tolkien: A Biography*, p. 49.

Chapter 6 – The Ribble Valley, Lancashire

1 *Letters*, p. 26; Shippey, *J.R.R. Tolkien: Author of the Century*, p. 61.

2 *Letters*, p. 391.

3 In his Foreword to Walter Edward Haigh's *A New Glossary of the Dialect of the Huddersfield District*

4 The principal source for information on the Pendle witches is *The Wonderful Discoverie of Witches in the Countie of Lancaster* by Thomas Potts published in 1613. Potts was the court clerk. Those interested in the subject should visit www.pendlewitches.co.uk from where this quote is transcribed.

5 Thomas, *Religion and the Decline of Magic*, p. 616; this paragraph and the preceding one draw on this book.

6 *The Monster and the Critics*, pp. 142–3.

Chapter 7 – Cheddar Gorge, Somerset; Brill, Buckinghamshire

1 *Letters*, p. 407.
2 *The War of the Ring*, p. 23.
3 See, for instance, *The Return of the Shadow*, p. 131.
4 *Letters*, p. 130.
5 http://www.brill.uk.net (also a source of other information in this chapter).
6 *Letters*, p. 376.
7 Melling, *The Place Names of Berkshire*, p. 806.

Chapter 8 – The Berkshire Downs

1 Much of the information in this chapter concerning the Berkshire Downs and their ancient monuments comes from two publications by Leslie Grinsell: *White Horse Hill and the Surrounding Country* (London, 1939) and *The Rollright Stones and their Folklore* (St Peter Port, 1977).
2 Shippey, *The Road to Middle Earth*, pp. 92–3.
3 Ibid., pp. 111–19; Shippey, *J.R.R. Tolkien: Author of the Century*, pp. 90–7.
4 *The Lays of Beleriand*, p. 141.
5 *Letters*, p. 218.
6 Ibid., p. 108.
7 *The Monster and the Critics*, p. 33.
8 Renfrew, *Archaeology and Language*, p. 19.
9 *Letters*, p. 65.
10 Simon Schama, *Landscape and Memory*, p. 142.
11 H.R. Loyn quoted in P.H. Sawyer, *From Roman Britain to Norman England*, p. 133.
12 Shippey, *The Road to Middle Earth*, p. 93.
13 Shippey, *J.R.R. Tolkien: Author of the Century*, p. 199.
14 *Archaeology*, issue 65, June 2002.

Chapter 9 – Rollright, Oxfordshire/Warwickshire

1 *Letters*, p. 130.
2 Interview with Philip Norman, *Sunday Times Magazine*, 15 January 1967.
3 *The Lost Road*, p. 38.

Chapter 10 – Fonthill, Wiltshire

1 *The Treason of Isengard*, pp. 417, 420.
2 *The Monster and the Critics*, p. 20.
3 Interview with Philip Norman, *Sunday Times Magazine*, 15 January 1967.
4 Shippey, *The Road to Middle Earth*, p. 119.

Bibliography

This bibliography is limited to the writings by Tolkien, interviews with Tolkien and books by other authors that I have used in writing *There and Back Again*. It is therefore by no means exhaustive.

Works of Fiction by J.R.R. Tolkien

In each case the year inside square brackets indicates publication of the first edition, while the second year given indicates publication by HarperCollins of the paperback edition consulted in the writing of this book.

The Hobbit, or There and Back Again ([1937]; 1999)
The Lord of the Rings ([1954–5]; 1995)
   1: *The Fellowship of the Ring*
   2: *The Two Towers*
   3: *The Return of the King*
The Silmarillion ([1977]; 1999)
Unfinished Tales ([1980]; 1998)
The History of Middle Earth, in 12 volumes, edited by Christopher Tolkien ([1983–96]; 2002)
   1: *The Book of Lost Tales, Part 1*
   2: *The Book of Lost Tales, Part 2*
   3: *The Lays of Beleriand*
   4: *The Shaping of Middle Earth*
   5: *The Lost Road, and Other Writings*
   6: *The Return of the Shadow*
   7: *The Treason of Isengard*

8: *The War of the Ring*
9: *Sauron Defeated*
10: *Morgoth's Ring*
11: *The War of the Jewels*
12: *The Peoples of Middle Earth*

Tales from the Perilous Realm (1997; 2002)
Which contains:
Farmer Giles of Ham [1949] and
The Adventures of Tom Bombadil, and Other Poems [1961]
Leaf By Niggle [1964]
Smith of Wootton Major [1967]

Other Works by J.R.R. Tolkien

'Philology, General Works' [reviews], in Sir Sidney Lee, F.S. Boas and C.H. Herford (eds), *The Year's Work in English Studies*, London: Oxford University Press, 1924

'Foreword', in Walter Edward Haigh, *A New Glossary of the Dialect of the Huddersfield District*, London: Oxford University Press, 1928

'Appendix 1: The Name 'Nodens', in R.E.M. Wheeler and T.V. Wheeler, *Report on the Excavation of the Prehistoric, Roman and Post Roman Site in Lyndey Park, Gloucestershire*, London: Society of Antiquaries, 1932

The Monster and the Critics, and Other Essays, London: HarperCollins, George Allen & Unwin [1983]; paperback edition 1997

Letters of J.R.R. Tolkien, edited by Humphrey Carpenter, London: George Allen & Unwin [1983]; paperback edition HarperCollins, 1995

Interviews with J.R.R. Tolkien

These appeared in the following publications:
New Worlds, Vol. 50, edited by Michael Moorcock, London: Compact Publishing, 1966
Oxford Mail (3 August 1966)
Glasgow Herald (6 August 1966)
Daily Express (22 November 1966)

Sunday Times (15 January 1967)
Scotsman (25 March 1967)
Birmingham Post (25 May 1968)
Sunday Times (2 January 1972)

Other Books Consulted

Anonymous, *Pearl, Cleanness, Patience, Sir Gawain and the Green Knight*, edited by A.C. Cawley and J.J. Anderson, London: Everyman 1985

Braudel, Fernand (tr. Siân Reynolds), *The Mediterranean in the Ancient World*, London: Allen Lane, 2001

Camden, William (tr. Philimon Holland), *Britannia*, London, 1610

Carpenter, Humphrey, *The Inklings*, London: George Allen & Unwin [1983]; paperback edition HarperCollins, 1997

Carpenter, Humphrey, *J.R.R. Tolkien: A* Biography, London: George Allen & Unwin [1977]; paperback edition George Allen & Unwin, 1978

Coe, Jonathan, *The Rotters' Club*, London: Viking [2001]; paperback edition Penguin Books, 2002

Du Maurier, Daphne, *Vanishing Cornwall*, London: Victor Gollancz, 1969

Fisher, D.J.V., *The Anglo-Saxon Age*, London: Longman, 1973

Fox, George, *Journal*, edited by Rufus M Jones, Richmond, Virginia, Friends United Press, 1976

Frere, Sheppard, *Britannia: A History of Roman Britain*, London: Routledge & Keegan Paul [1967]; paperback edition Pimlico, 1991

Gelling, Margaret, *The Place Names of Berkshire*, Cambridge: English Place Name Society, 1976

Grinsell, L.V, *White Horse Hill and the Surrounding Countryside*, London: St Catherine Press, 1939

Grinsell, L.V., *The Rollright Stones and their Folklore*, St Peter Port: Toucan Press, 1977

Hamer, Richard (ed.), *A Choice of Anglo-Saxon Verse*, London: Faber & Faber, 1970

Hanbury-Tenison, Robin (ed.), *The Oxford Book of Exploration*, London: Oxford University Press, 1993

Lobdell, Jared (ed.), *A Tolkien Compass*, La Salle, IL: Open Court, 1974

The Mercia Movement *The Mercia Manifesto* Cotes Heath, Stafford: Witan Books, 1997

Murray, Les, *Selected Poems*, Manchester: Carcanet, 1986

Pound, Ezra, *Selected Poems,*London: Faber & Faber, 1981

P.H. Sawyer, *From Roman Britain to Norman England*, London: Routledge, 1998

Schama, Simon, *Landscape and Memory*, London: HarperCollins [1995]; paperback edition Fontana Press, 1996

Shippey, Tom, *The Road to Middle Earth*, London: George Allen & Unwin [1982, paperback edition Grafton, 1992]

Shippey, Tom, *J.R.R. Tolkien: Author of the Century*, London: [2000], paperback edition, HarperCollins, 2001

Smith, Geoffrey Bache, *A Spring Harvest*, London: Erskine Macdonald, 1918

Thomas, Sir Keith, *Religion and the Decline of Magic: Studies in Popular Beliefs in Sixteenth- and Seventeenth-Century England*, London: Weidenfeld & Nicolson [1971], paperback edition Penguin Books, 1988